HEAVEN MY BLANKET, EARTH MY PILLOW

HEAVEN MY BLANKET, EARTH MY PILLOW

Poems by
YANG WAN-LI

TRANSLATED AND INTRODUCED BY
JONATHAN CHAVES

WHITE PINE PRESS • BUFFALO, NEW YORK

This book was originally published by John Weatherhill, Inc.

Individual poems in this collection have appeared previously in the fol-
lowing magazines: *The Columbia Review, Granite, The Hudson Review, The
Malahat review, Mademoiselle, New Letters,* and *Transpacific.*

Publication of this book was made possible, in part, with public funds
from the New York State Council on the Arts, a State Agency.

First Edition

Library of Congress Control Number: 2004109163

Published by
White Pine Press
P.O. Box 236
Buffalo, New York 14201
www.whitepine.org

For Burton Watson,
teacher, inspiration

CONTENTS

TRANSLATOR'S INTRODUCTION / 9

The Life and Career of Yang Wan-li / 12

The Poetry of the Sung Dynasty / 17

The Poetry of Yang Wan-li / 26

On the Relationship of Poetry and Painting in China / 40

A NOTE ON THE TRANSLATIONS / 45

ACKNOWLEDGMENTS / 46

POEMS BY YANG WAN-LI / 47

NOTES ON THE ILLUSTRATIONS / 124

BIOGRAPHICAL NOTE / 125

Translator's Introduction

"In my life I have loved nothing else—I have loved only literature, as other men love beautiful women. And I have especially loved poetry." These words were written by Yang Wan-li, who lived in China during the Southern Sung dynasty (A.D. 1127-1279), a period when the Chinese suffered constantly the threat of invasion by northern nomads. First the Jurchens overran northern China, establishing the Chin dynasty in 1126 and forcing the Sung court to transfer its capital to the southern city of Hangchow. Later came the Mongols, who finally overthrew the Sung in 1279 and founded their own Yuan dynasty.

Despite the personal insecurity that the Chinese must have experienced during these turbulent years, Southern Sung literature and art are often characterized by a wistful calm, a softness that seems surprising at first. A classic expression of this mood might be the small album-leaf painting by Ma Yuan that appears on page ?? of this book. Ma Yuan (flourished c. 1190-1230), known as "One-corner Ma" for his characteristic compositional technique of concentrating his subject matter in one corner of a painting, here depicts a scholar sitting in contemplation of a mist-filled void. The bank or terrace on which the scholar sits is a tiny portion of the world, though vast distances are suggested by the rich emptiness. The Chinese of the Southern Sung had created at Hangchow a refuge of elegant solitude from which they gazed longingly toward the north, and in this quiet setting they were able to enjoy the beauties of bird, rock, and stream.

THE LIFE AND CAREER OF YANG WAN-LI

Yang Wan-li's life was relatively uneventful, the life of a typical Chinese scholar-bureaucrat moving from one official post to another. He was born in Chi-shui Subprefecture in Kiangsi in 1127, the very year that the Sung court was forced to flee to the south. Nothing is known about his parents, although in a short book of comments on literature, Yang speaks of several of his ancestors as having been good poets. Yang's life apparently began in poverty. By the time he was twenty he was studying seriously, preparing himself for the arduous series of examinations that would qualify him for a career in the bureaucracy. "At that time," he later wrote, "I would always close my study door, chant aloud from my books, and devote myself completely to literature as if I were mad or deluded, exhausted or ill." Yang had to emphasize literature because the composition of poetry was one of the important criteria by which civil-service candidates were judged. In 1154, upon passing the final and highest examination, Yang earned the *chin-shih*, or doctoral degree, which would allow him to begin his career as an official of the state.

Yang's first post upon admission to the bureaucracy was administrator of finances of Kan-chou Prefecture. In 1159, he was transferred to Ling-ling Subprefecture in Hunan. While there, he tried three times to see the official Chang Chün (d. 1164), who had been exiled from the capital because of his advocacy of an aggressive policy toward the Chin dynasty in the north. Finally, Yang wrote Chang a letter, and was granted an audience. Chang urged the young Yang to practice "rectifying the mind" and "making one's thoughts sincere," expressions from the Confucian text *The Great Learning*. Deeply impressed, Yang later took Ch'eng-chai (Studio of Sincerity) as his *hao*, or nom de plume.

In the Chinese system of government, a young official's personal relationships with senior bureaucrats were often a determining factor in the advancement of his career, and Yang's association with Chang Chün led to his first appointment in the capital. When Emperor Hsiao-tsung ascended the throne in 1163, Chang was recalled from exile to become a high-ranking official at the new emperor's court. Remembering Yang, he recommended the younger scholar-official for promotion. Yang was appointed professor of Lin-an Prefecture, but was unable to take up the post because his father died and he had to return home to Chi-shui to observe the obligatory "three year" mourning period. According to the usual custom, however, Yang actually spent only two full years and an additional three months—symbolic of the third year—in mourning.

Yang received further official recognition in 1167, when he submitted to the throne his famous memorial entitled *Ch'ien lü ts'e* (A Thousand Concerns). In this work Yang advocated the strong defense of the Huai River, the existing border separating the Chin to the north and the Sung to the south. "If the Huai is crossed," he wrote, "it will be difficult to defend the Yangtze." The commissioner of military affairs, Yü Yün-wen (d. 1174), and the prime minister, Ch'en Chün-ch'ing (d. 1186), were sufficiently impressed by the *Ch'ien Lü ts'e* to have Yang promoted to the position of professor of the Directorate of Education. While holding this office, Yang had an opportunity to repay Chang Chün (albeit posthumously) for his kindnesses by courageously supporting Chang's son, Chang Ch'ih (1133-80), in his protest against the appointment of a corrupt official who had attained power only because he was a distaff relative of the emperor.

After occupying a succession of posts in both the capital and the provinces, Yang was sent to Kwangtung as administrator of tea and salt taxes and later as judiciary intendant. In 1181, the bandit Shen Shih descended on Kwangtung with a horde of thieves from Fukien, and as a ranking local official Yang was called upon to defend the city. Leading a group of government troops, he successfully routed the robber band. This experience inspired one of his rare poems on a social theme:

One night, the Fukien robbers eyed Kwangtung;

by morning, the Southern armies had all moved eastward.
The shouts of the troops shook cliffs and valleys;
banners flapped briskly in the cold wind.
Leopards and tigers gathered from all sides;
the rebel leaders were wiped out with a laugh.
Petty men, like a pack of rats—
beating them was no great task.

Yang's mother died in 1182, apparently of a pulmonary ailment for which she had been treated years before. Once again, Yang retired from office to observe the period of mourning. He returned to the capital two years later to become assistant director, subsequently director, of the Bureau of Administration. The prime minister, Wang Huai (1126-89), greatly valuing Yang's judgment, asked him to submit a list of gifted men to be considered for promotion. Yang named sixty men, beginning with Chu Hsi (1130-1200), the foremost Neo-Confucian philosopher of his time, who had been introduced to Yang by Chang Ch'ih. Also included in the list was Hsiao Te-tsao (flourished c. 1147), an important poet.

Despite this recognition of Yang's judgment of character, he was not to rise as high in government as he deserved. His tendency to express his feelings honestly and directly brought him into conflict with powerful forces at court and at times jeopardized his career. The most serious instance occurred in 1188, when Yang criticized the influential official Hung Mai (1123-1202) with the words: "He pointed to a deer and called it a horse." Yang was comparing Hung Mai with Chao Kao, the infamous eunuch of the Ch'in dynasty (221-206 B.C.) who exercised total authority under Erh-shih Huang-ti, the "Second Emperor" of the Ch'in. So great was Chao's power that when he pointed to a deer and called it a horse, no one dared contradict him. The implication for the Southern Sung emperor Hsiao-tsung was that Yang was comparing him with the ineffectual Second Emperor. Enraged at what he considered lese majesty on Yang's part, the emperor appointed Yang to the post of prefect of Yün-chou Prefecture in Kiangsi, an action which amounted to banishment from the capital.

Another unfortunate side effect of this affair was the disloyalty of Yang's friend Chou Pi-ta (*1126-1204*), an important poet and critic who greatly admired Yang's writing. According to Yang's biography in the *Sung shih* (the official history of the Sung dynasty), when Emperor Hsiao-tsung asked Chou what he thought of Yang, Chou "had nothing good to say, and from this time on, Yang was never again employed [in a high office by Hsiao-tsung]." No doubt intimidated by the emperor, Chou was probably afraid to express his true feelings about his friend.

When Emperor Kuang-tsung came to the throne in *1189*, Yang was recalled to the capital and appointed to the highest office he was to attain during his official career, director of the Imperial Library. This post held the rank 4-A in a system of nine twofold ranks, I-A being the highest. But in the following year, the ex-emperor Hsiao-tsung discovered that Yang was back in the capital and asked, "Why is Yang Wan-li still around here?" When Kuang-tsung did not immediately understand the implication of his father's angry question, Hsiao-tsung explained: "In one of his memorials he compared me with the Second Emperor of the Ch'in dynasty!"

Once again, Yang was sent away from the capital, this time to serve as assistant commissioner of transportation for Chiang-tung. He was not without supporters, however. Before he was sent to Chiang-tung, the scholar Ni Ssu (*1147-1220*) petitioned that he be kept at court. To little avail, Ni praised Yang, saying: "In learning and literary ability he is, of course, outstanding. But it is particularly difficult to find a man who is both so resolute and so perspicacious. When confronted with a situation, he acts fearlessly. His thinking has aided the country. Such is his loyalty!"

Yang Wan-li's official career ended in *1192* when, at the age of sixty-five, he retired to his birthplace in Chi-shui because of his opposition to the use of metal currency in the Chiang-nan region, the area south of the Yangtze River. He was summoned to the capital in *1195*, and again in *1205*, but declined to go. The court nevertheless granted him honorary titles, the highest being Scholar of the Pao-mo Pavilion, in *1206*.

While living in retirement, Yang was asked by the notorious Han T'o-chou, the most powerful official of the time, to write an essay about a new garden which Han was constructing. Yang refused, and the essay was finally written by the great poet Lu Yu (1125-1209). Yang, a friend of Lu's, chided Lu in an elegant couplet:

> A poet with the genius of a Li or a Tu,
>> whales churning up the ocean,
> Should not envy the dragons
>> who gather at Phoenix Pond.

Yang means that Lu, a poet of the stature of Li Po and Tu Fu, the two most esteemed poets of the T'ang dynasty, should not have curried favor with Han T'o-chou and other powerful but unsavory officials at the court (the "dragons who gather at Phoenix Pond").

In 1206, Han T'o-chou violated the Chin-Sung peace treaty and attacked the Chin forces. According to the official account of Yang Wan-li's life in the *Sung shih*, Yang died of grief and anger in this same year, when he learned of this untimely move. He must already have been in a greatly weakened condition, however, for many of his later poems speak of recurring illnesses.

Yang was survived by his wife, three sons, and a daughter. Yang's wife, the daughter of the well-known scholar Lo Fu, was by all accounts a remarkable woman. She breast-fed her children herself, refusing to follow the common practice of using wet nurses. "What sort of person would I be," she is reported to have said, "if I deprived other children to feed my own?" An anecdote told by Lo Ta-ching gives a further hint of her strength of character: "Yang's wife, nee Lo, when she was over seventy, would rise at the crack of dawn during the cold months. She would go to the kitchen, make a pot of gruel, and serve it to all the servants, only then allowing them to perform their duties. Her son Tung-shan [Yang Chang-ju, the eldest son] reproached her, 'Why do you endure such hardship when it is this cold?' She replied, 'The servants are also people. It is chilly early in the morning. Only if they have something hot in their stomachs will they be able to do their work.'"

As is true of many other Chinese poets, little of Yang's personality shines through the few facts and anecdotes that are available to us. His poems are much more meaningful in this respect than any of the biographical material. Also revealing are poems written about him by other men, such as this one by his contemporary Ko T'ien-min:

> I have never known him to be given a high official post;
> I have only known him to endure hunger for seventy years.
> Yet his back is strong as iron, his mind is firm as stone;
> He has never bent his knee or knit his brow.
> Nor has he merely dabbled in literature—
> He has written poems.

THE POETRY OF THE SUNG DYNASTY

By now, most interested Western readers have some familiarity with the works of the great poets of the T'ang dynasty (618-906): Wang Wei, Li Po, Tu Fu, and Po Chü-i. But the literary achievements of the Sung dynasty are still largely unknown. In the Sung, as in the T'ang, the most important poetic form was the classic *shih*, in which with few exceptions every line of a given poem consists of five or seven characters, each of them monosyllabic. The Sung also saw the development of the *tz'u*, or lyric, in which lines of differing length occur. Although introduced during the T'ang, the *tz'u* form did not really come into its own until the Sung. Yang Wan-li wrote a number of *tz'u*, but the major portion of his verse is in the *shih* form.

Schools of poetry, a phenomenon that had not been of much importance during the T'ang, took a strong hold over the Sung literary world. Early during the Northern Sung there were three major groups of poets whose works were classified by critics as the Hsi-k'un style, the Po Chü-i style, and the Late T'ang style. The Hsi-k'un school produced elegant, highly allusive verse which, although it attained great popularity at the very beginning of the eleventh century, was dismissed by virtually all later critics for its artificiality.

Po Chü-i (772-846), the famous T'ang poet, wrote poetry characterized by social concern, the depiction of everyday experience, and simplicity of diction. The most important of the early Northern Sung poets who emulated his style was Wang Yü-ch'eng (954-1001). As the first truly major poet of the new dynasty, Wang has been considered the father of Sung poetry, and he was conscious of the need to create a revitalized poetics for the Sung. "If I remain silent," he wrote, "people of later generations who read my collection will say there were no poets in the Sung dynasty." Wang's best poems achieve great power through the use of diction that often approaches colloquial directness. In this he foreshadows Yang Wan-li, who has come to be known as the *pai-hua shih-jen* (colloquial poet). As an example of the strength of Wang's colloquial diction, here is one of his finest works, the "Song of the Crow Pecking at My Scarred Donkey." The poem was written in 992, one year after Wang had been exiled to Shang-chou Prefecture in Shensi at the age of thirty-eight:

> Old crow of Shang Mountain, you are cruel!
> Beak longer than a spike, sharper than an arrow.
> Go gather bugs or peck at eggs—
> why must you harm this poor scarred beast of mine?
> Since I was exiled to Shang-yu last year,
> there has only been this one lame donkey to move my
> > things.
> We climbed the Ch'in Mountains and the Ch'an to get here;
> he carried a hundred volumes for me on his back.
> The ropes cut his skin to the spine, the scar reached his
> > belly;
> now with half a year's healing he's nearly well again.
> But yesterday the crow suddenly swooped down,
> and pecked through his wound to get the living flesh.
> The donkey brayed, my servant cried out,
> and the crow flew away!
> Perched on the roof he preened his feathers and scraped his
> > beak

There was nothing my donkey and my servant could do
without a crossbow to shoot or nets to spread.
But Shang Mountain has many birds of prey—
I'll ask our neighbor to lend me his autumn hawk.
With claws of iron and hooked talons
he'll snap the crow's neck and feed on his brain!
And this won't serve only to fill his empty gut;
No! It's revenge for my donkey's pain.

The third of the early Northern Sung styles, the "Late T'ang," derived from the poetry of Chia Tao (c. 793-c. 865) and his followers. The poems of these men were almost always written in strict, regulated verse forms of four or eight lines, and were usually intimate landscape poems free of the bookish allusions and obscure expressions that marred the Hsi-k'un style. Typical of the early Northern Sung poets who wrote in this mode was Lin Pu (967-1028), whose work is well represented by "An Autumn Day—Leisurely Boating on West Lake":

The water's breath mingles with reflected mountains;
autumn has come to the vast sky.
I joy to see temples hidden deep in the forest,
regret the broken silence when my boat moves from the
        shore.
Sparse reeds are snapping, though it isn't cold yet;
a rainbow's fragment arches in the setting sun.
Which way now to my little hut?
The fishermen's songs bring thoughts of home.

The poet has quieted his mind and entered a meditative state in which he is the perfect perceiver of such phenomena as the snapping of reeds and a fragmentary rainbow. This attention to the ephemeral manifestations of nature must have appealed to Yang Wan-li, who frequently expressed his admiration for Late T'ang poetry:

> Who will enjoy with me
>> the strange flavor of Late T'ang?
> Recent poets have held Late T'ang in contempt!

It was only with the great poets of the eleventh century that Northern Sung poetry really came into its own, and was less dominated by the pervasive influence of the T'ang. The development of a new style was largely the achievement of two men, both major figures in the intellectual and artistic worlds of their time, Mei Yao-ch'en (1002-60) and Ou-yang Hsiu (1007-72).

Mei and Ou-yang were close friends, and they constantly exchanged poems. Of the two, Mei was the more brilliant poet, although Ou-yang has become more famous because of his distinguished career as a statesman and thinker. Mei's work is too varied and rich to be summarized easily. That he was a master of objective description is to be seen in his poems on archaeological objects. But he also wrote extremely moving poems of personal emotion. Here, for example, is "The Year Wu-tzu, First Month, Night of the Twenty-sixth: A Dream," a poem inspired by a dream of his first wife, who had died four years earlier, Mei having since remarried:

> Two years now since my second marriage;
> in all that time, I've never dreamed of her.
> Last night I saw her face again;
> midnight was a painful hour.
> The dark lamp glowed with a feeble light,
> silently glimmering on the rafters.
> And the unfeeling snow that beat against my window
> was whirled to a frenzy by the wind.

The generation following Mei produced the most outstanding poets of the Northern Sung dynasty. Wang Yu-ch'eng, Mei Yao-ch'en, and Ou-yang Hsiu had prepared the way for a great flourishing of poetry in the second half of the eleventh century. Four poets in particular dominated the literary scene at this time: Wang An-shih, Su Shih, Huang T'ing-chien, and Ch'en Shih-tao.

Wang An-shih (*1021-86*) rose to become prime minister under Emperor Shen-tsung (reigned *1069-85*), and the series of radical economic policies that he instituted have made him one of the most controversial statesmen in Chinese history. As a poet, Wang was best known for his finely crafted four-line poems (*chüeh-chü*) with seven characters in each line, often depicting quiet scenes of the Late T'ang type. Yang Wan-li acknowledged Wang as one of the poets by whom he was most influenced, referring particularly to his seven-character *chüeh chü*. Here is "The River Mouth at Chiang-ning," one of Wang An-shih's better-known poems:

> We lower sail in the evening moonlight, and moor at the
> river mouth.
> The lights are out at the little inn; the doors are being
> closed.
> A half-dead maple juts out from the sandy bank—
> we can still see the marks where we moored last year.

The man who is usually considered the greatest Sung poet is Su Shih (*1037-1101*), also known as Su Tung-p'o. Su is also famous as a painter and calligrapher. His circle of friends included the most distinguished writers and artists of the time, and among them they virtually created the image of the Sung *wen-len* (scholar-poet-artist). Characteristic of the way in which they brought the arts together is a painting entitled *Herdboy with Bamboo and Rock*, jointly painted by Su Tung-p'o and the famous figure painter Li Kung-lin (c. *1040-1106*). Huang T'ing-chien (*1045-1105*) then described the painting in a poem, preceded by a brief prose preface:

> Su Tung-p'o painted a clump of bamboo and a fantastic
> rock. Li Kung-lin added a slope in the foreground and a
> herdboy riding a water buffalo. The picture, full of life, has
> inspired these playful verses:

Here's a little craggy rock in a wild place,
shadowed by green bamboo.
A herdboy, wielding a three-foot stick,
drives his lumbering old water buffalo.
I love the rock.
Don't let the buffalo rub his horns on it.
Well, all right, let him rub his horns—
but if he gets too rough, he'll break the bamboo.

When Su Tung-p'o passed the *chin-shih* examination in 1057, one of the examiners was Mei Yao-ch'en. Su was inspired by Mei, both as a man and as a poet, and like Mei he wrote poetry in a remarkable variety of modes. At his best, he could attain passionate intensity, as in the following poem, "The Jade Stream Pavilion at K'ai-hsien Temple." (The Ch'in Kao referred to in the fourth line from the end was a Taoist immortal who rode off into a river on the back of a huge carp, never to return.)

The red sun sinks behind high cliffs.
A sad wind is blowing through the chasm.
This is where Jade Gorge splits wide open
and two white dragons plunge down,
their wild spittle flying like snowflakes.
The sky trembles in an old pond—
 water, smooth and quiet,
flows through the Valley of Twin Rocks.

I have come here, and I don't want to leave:
the moon is rising east of the natural bridge,
vast tower of white silver,
 silent palace of crystal.
I want to follow Ch'in Kao
and ride the red carp,
or hold a white lotus in my hand
and dive deep into cool water.

"Su Tung-p'o," wrote Yang Wan-li, "was even crazier than I."

Despite his association with Su Tung-p'o, Huang T'ing-chien was a very different kind of poet. The playfulness of the poem on the painting by Su and Li Kung-lin is unusual: most of Huang's work seems dry in tone and is often quite allusive, requiring heavy annotation. His diction is frequently dense in texture. In all these respects he differs from Yang Wan-li, and yet Yang admired him, expressing the wish in an early poem that his poetry might someday be as good as Huang's.

Ch'en Shih-tao (*1053-1102*), another disciple of Su Tung p'o's, was also known for his intense concern with craftsmanship for its own sake. Although he occasionally breaks through to passionate expression, most of his work strikes the modern reader as dry and uninteresting. Both Huang and Ch'en appear to have been admired primarily for their technical finesse and virtuosity, and many later Sung poets, including Yang Wan-li, began to write by emulating the works of these two men and their followers. Because Huang came from Chiang-hsi (Kiangsi), he and Ch'en, together with twenty-four other poets, were grouped together as the "Chiang-hsi school" in a list compiled by the poet Lü Chü-jen (*1137-81*).

The year *1127*, which was the year of Yang Wan-li's birth marked the beginning of the Southern Sung dynasty. With the political change, there was a corresponding cultural transition. In painting, the grandiose monumentality of much of Northern Sung art gave way to the intimate album leaves of Ma Yuan and his followers, and to the brilliant but also small-scaled ink paintings of the Ch'an (Zen) Buddhist painters.

As regards poetry, partly because of the separate development of the *tz'u* form, the transition is not easily summarized. It can be said, however, that the scholarly intellectualism of the influential Chiang-hsi school waned in favor of a more intimate style on the part of the most important Southern Sung poets writing in the classic *shih* form. Critics usually speak of the "Four Great Masters of the Southern Sung," all of whom were close contemporaries and friends, frequently exchanging poetry with each other. In a preface to the collected works of the poet Hsiao Te-tsao (fl. c. *1147*), Yang Wan-li wrote concerning the four masters: "I have discussed the recent poets and spoken of the fresh newness of Fan Ch'eng-ta, the bland simplicity of Yu Mao, the ample richness of Lu Yu, and the masterly skill of Hsiao Te-tsao. I hold all of them in awe."

Later, Yang himself replaced Hsiao as one of the four masters. And since the collections of Hsiao and Yu Mao have been lost, Southern Sung *shih* poetry is now dominated for us by three men: Yang, Fan Ch'eng-ta, and Lu Yu.

Lu Yu (1125-1209), with some ten thousand poems to his name, is China's most prolific poet. He is often called the "patriotic poet" because of the moving poems in which he expresses his desire to drive out the Chin invaders and recapture northern China for the Sung. But Lu was transferred to a post in Szechwan in western China, far from the battle-front. Frustrated in his military aspirations, he was forced to come to terms with his actual identity as a scholar-poet, rather than as the victorious general he became in his dreams. Lu consoled himself with poetry. There he was able to strike a beautiful ironic balance, as in such poems as "Light Rain on the Road to Sword Gate," written as he journeyed to Szechwan to take up his post:

> Wine stains and mud mottle my coat.
> As I travel on, my heart breaks with every scene.
> It looks as if I'm a poet at last,
> riding my donkey through Sword Gate in the drizzling rain.

Lu Yu and Yang Wan-li were good friends and admired each other's work. "I am not as good as Ch'eng-chai [Yang Wan-li]," wrote Lu, "everyone is agreed on this." The incident of the essay on the Han T'o-chou garden, which Lu composed after Yang's refusal, seems to have created some tension between the two poets, and in the later chapters of Yang's collected works there are no poems to Lu.

Fan Ch'eng-ta (1126-93), also a friend of Yang's, asked him to write the preface to his collected works. Like Yang, Fan earned his *chin-shih* degree in 1154, and this in itself created a special bond between them: men who received their degrees in the same year often became lifelong friends. Fan is best known for a cycle of sixty *chüch-chü* poems on farm life, arranged according to season. The relaxed tone of these vignettes of rural life can be sensed in one of the summer poems:

> A sweating traveler, covered with dust,
> stops at my house for some fresh water.
> "Sit down on the big rock near the gate.
> It's noon, and there's a breeze in the willows."

Fan was also capable of writing social-protest poetry of great power. Although Yang's concern about the political realities of his time is demonstrated by his famous memorial of 1167, *A Thousand Concerns*, politics and social protest play a very slight role in his poetry. But one of Fan's protest poems will be given here as an example of a very important type; "Tax Song" denounces the conditions that destroyed peasant families and condemned them to a life of extreme poverty and starvation:

> Autumn rains have swamped the old farmer's fields,
> the river flows where the bank used to be.
> "I'm a hired man now, always hungry;
> I'll never be able to pay the rice tax this year!
> Since the new magistrate took office,
> they've been remitting our taxes with yellow papers,
>   then collecting them with white papers.
> I sold my clothes to pay the tax;
> my bones froze, but I didn't go to jail.
> Last year I ran out of clothes;
>   there was nothing to sell but my family.
> I said goodbye to my eldest daughter at the crossroads.
> My second daughter got engaged this year,
> but I'll have to sell her too, for bushels and pecks.
> There's still a third daughter in the house—
> I'm not worrying about next year's taxes."

In general, the Sung poets were more prolific than their predecessors of the T'ang dynasty. Lu Yu wrote some ten thousand poems, an astonishing figure. Yang Wan-li was the next most prolific, with a total of about 4,200 poems in his collected writings; this sum does not include over a thousand early poems that Yang burned in 1162, when he appears to have suffered some kind of artistic crisis. Yang's complete works comprise a volume of 130 *chüan* (chapters), as well as an important commentary on the *I Ching* (The Book of Changes), which took him seventeen years to write.

In a poem praising Yang, his friend Lou Yueh (*1137-1213*) wrote:

> You have written a book of poems
> > for each office you have held,
> transmitting nearly a thousand *chüan!*

"Yang Wan-li wrote a book of poems for each office he held," echoed the critic Fang Hui (*1227-1306*), "and each book represented a change of style."

Yang compiled a total of nine collections: *Chiang-hu* (Rivers and Lakes), including poems written during the years 1162-77; *Ching-ch'i* (Poems from Ching-ch'i), 1178-79; *Hsi-kuei* (Return to the West), 1179-80; *Nan-hai* (South Seas), 1180-82; *Ch'ao-t'ien* (Going to Court), 1184-87 (Yang was ill in 1183, and seems to have written no poems); *Chiang-hsi tao-yüan* (The Taoist Retreat West of the River), 1188-89; *Ch'ao-t'ien hsu* (Going to Court Again), 1190; *Chiang-tung* (East of the River), 1190-92; and *T'ui-hsiu* (In Retirement), 1192 and after.

Included among Yang's writings is a short book called *Ch'eng-chai shih-hua* (Ch'eng-chai's [Yang Wan-li's] Comments on Poetry). Despite its title, however, this book is disappointing as a source for his ideas about his art. It seems to reflect Yang's concerns as a young poet learning his craft; there is much discussion of allusion to old poetry and the use of standard images. "A beginner in the writing of poetry," he tells us, "must study the best phrases of the ancients, whether two words or three." This is a far cry from Yang's later independence and insistence on the creation of a unique, personal style.

The poets Yang mentions most frequently in the *Ch'eng-chai shih-hua* are Tu Fu, Li Po, and Han Yü (768-824) of the T'ang, and Wang An-shih, Huang T'ing-chien, and Su Tung-p'o of the Sung. The book was appraised by the Ch'ing scholar Chi Yün (1724–1805): "This work is entitled *Comments on Poetry*, but it has more entries dealing with prose than with poetry. It also touches upon humorous anecdotes and miscellaneous matters; Sung 'comments on poetry' are often like this."

Yang offers far more insight into his feelings about poetry in the important preface he wrote to his second collection, the *Ching-ch'i*. This preface, dated 1187, is worth translating in full:

"I began my practice of poetry by studying the poets of the Chiang-hsi school; then I studied the five-character regulated verse of Hou-shan [Ch'en Shih-tao]. Then I studied the seven-character *chüeh-chü* of Old Man Pan-shan [Wang An-shih]; and finally I studied the *chüeh-chü* of the [Late] T'ang poets. But the harder I studied, the fewer poems I wrote. I complained about this several times to Lin Ch'ien-chih [Lin Kuang-chiao, 1114–78, a philosopher and poet], and he said, 'When you select so carefully the poets you wish to emulate, and when it is so hard to master their styles, how can you help writing very little?' I sighed and said, 'Am I alone in this? Poets show different symptoms, but these all come from the same source.' For I had written as few as 582 poems in the period 1162 to 1177.

"That summer [1177] I went to Ching-ch'i to become governor there. When I arrived, what with examining documents and putting the tax system in order, I had no time for anything else. Ideas for poems came to me, but I had no time to write them down. On New Year's Day, 1178, I was on holiday and had few official duties, so I was able to write poetry. Suddenly, I felt as if enlightenment had come, and I thereupon said goodbye to the T'ang poets, Wang, Ch'en, and the poets of the Chiang-hsi school, not daring to study them again, and I felt very happy. I had my son write down the poems as I recited them; they came flowing out, without the laborious grinding of former days.

"From that time on, whenever afternoon came and the various officials went away leaving the courtyard empty, I would take a fan, walk in the back yard, climb the old city wall, pluck chrysanthemums, and fondle bamboo. The ten thousand images of nature would present themselves to me as material for poems; I would motion them away but they kept coming, and before I had written them down others would follow directly behind. I no longer felt that it was hard to write poetry. The 'poet's disease' seemed about to leave me. At this time, not only was it easier to write poetry, but governing my province seemed to grow easier, too!

"On the thirtieth day of the second month of the following year [1179], my successor arrived. I handed over the insignia of office and left. When I put together what I had written during the previous fourteen months, I found that there were 492 poems in all. But I did not dare to take them out and show them to people.

"This year I am working in the central government. My friend Chung Chiang-chih wrote me a letter from the Huai River, saying: 'Ching-ch'i has recently changed governors. It may have been easy for you to govern the place, but now the difficulty has increased more than tenfold. Could you perhaps make public your Ching-ch'i poems?' I laughed copied them out, and sent them to him."

Yang specifies the poets who influenced him most, but goes on to proclaim the importance of finding his own, personal style. As a young poet, Yang had followed his own advice in the *Ch'eng-chai shih-hua* and studied closely the great masters. But he was able to find happiness as a poet only when he stopped imitating others and achieved a style of his own. Yang's earlier, imitative works are included in his first collection, the *Chiang-hu*. In the preface to that work he wrote: "When I was young I wrote over a thousand poems, but in the seventh month of the year *jen-wu* of the Shao-hsing period [1162], I burned them all. For the most part, they were written in the Chiang-hsi style. The poems which have been preserved in the Chiang-hu collection are based on the styles of Ch'en Shih-tao, Wang An-shih, and the Late T'ang poets."

Having outgrown his early imitativeness, Yang became a champion of individuality in poetic style. "You ask me what to take as a model [*fa*] for writing good verses," he wrote in a poem addressed to a Taoist priest. "There is no model, there is no begging bowl, nor is there a robe." The begging bowl and robe he refers to were symbols of the transmission of the teaching in a Buddhist sect. The word *fa*, translated "model" here, is also the Chinese translation of the Sanskrit word *dharma*, meaning "law," "doctrine," or "teaching." Paraphrasing Yang's admonitions, a poet must sever his ties with the traditions of the past. Although he learns his craft by mastering these traditions, he must find a style of his own. The same idea is expressed in another poem:

> I'd be ashamed to continue a school,
> > or carry on a sect.
> Each writer must form his own style,
> > with a beauty all its own.
> Don't rest your feet beneath the hedge
> > of Huang and Ch'en.
> Move ahead of the ranks of T'ao and Hsich.

Huang T'ing-chien, Ch'en Shih-tao, T'ao Ch'ien (364–427), and Hsieh Ling-yün (385–433) were all poets Yang admired. But he insisted that the true poet should free himself even of the influence of such giants as these.

When a poet begins to write in a style of his own, he will find that poetry comes naturally to him, that he need no longer work over each line again and again. His poems begin "flowing out, without the laborious grinding of former days." He now finds his inspiration in nature, rather than in the poetry of the past. Yang's poem "Going Down the Heng Mountain Rapids, Gazing at Gold Flower Mountain" is based on this concept:

> Mountain thoughts, river feelings—
> > never betray them.
> Rain forms, sky patterns are always beautiful.
> "Closing the door and searching for verses"
> > is not the way of poetry.
> It is only when you travel that poems will come
> > naturally.

It was Ch'en Shih-tao of the Chiang-hsi school who was said to "close the door and search for verses"—that is, devote himself to the *craft* of poetry, working in the solitude of his studio. Yang repudiates the self-conscious technical mastery of the Chiang-hsi poets, replacing it with the inspiration of nature. Now the poem seems to search the poet out rather than the poet the poem, as in Yang's "Written on a Cold Evening":

> The poet must work with brush and paper,
> but this is not what makes the poem.
> A man doesn't go in search of a poem—
> the poem comes in search of him.

Yang's emphasis on the poet's development of a personal style may have been influenced by Ch'an (Zen) Buddhism, with its advocacy of enlightenment attained through individual effort. Ch'an first appeared in the T'ang dynasty, but flourished during the Sung as well. The two most popular collections of Ch'an anecdotes called *kung-an* (Japanese, *koan*) were compiled in 1125 and 1228, dates which, significantly, encompass Yang's life. Yang himself uses certain Chian terminology in a number of his poems. For example, in "Reading the Poetry of the T'ang Masters and Pan-shan," he writes:

> Although Pan-shan could be penetrating [ts'an-t'ou]
> the T'ang masters were a mountain pass beyond him.

Ts'an-t'ou is a Ch'an term meaning "deeply penetrating" in the sense of having special insight. Even more explicitly, Yang writes in another poem:

> Would you know how poets study the Chiang-hsi school?
> Just as Ch'an adepts study Ts'ao-ch'i.

Ts'ao-ch'i was the site of a temple where Hui-neng (d. 713), the famous Sixth Patriarch of Ch'an, taught. The reference to the Chiang-hsi school seems strange in this context, but Yang may be suggesting that many students of Ch'an do not fully understand the freedom that comes with enlightenment, and approach Ch'an as if it were merely another sect, just as poets wrongly tie themselves to a particular school of poetry. Passages such as these suggest that Yang may have influenced Yen Yü (c. 1200), author of the well-known *Ts'ang-lang shih-hua* (Ts'ang-lang's Comments on Poetry), which states that "discussing poetry is like discussing Ch'an."

Probably the most trenchant of Yang's own Ch'an-influenced statements on poetry is found in his introduction to a collection of poems by his contemporary Liu Ying-shih:

> Now, what is poetry?
> If you say it is simply a matter of words,
> I will say a good poet gets rid of words.
> If you say it is simply a matter of meaning,
> I will say a good poet gets rid of meaning.
> "But," you ask, "without words and without meaning,
>   where is the poetry?"
> To this I reply: "Get rid of words and get rid of meaning,
>   and there is still poetry."

It is not surprising that the poet and critic Liu K'o-chuang (1187-1269) considered Yang to be a "Ch'an patriarch" in the development of Sung poetry: "In making an analogy to the Ch'an sect, Huang T'ing-chien may be considered the First Patriarch. Lü Pen-chung [1084-1138] and Tseng Chi [1084–1166] were the Southern and Northern schools [into which Ch'an was traditionally divided]. Yang Wan-li appeared on the scene somewhat later. He was Lin-chi [founder of the Lin-chi sect, known in Japanese Zen as Rinzai] and Te-shan [782-865, a great Ch'an monk]."

Yang's experience of Buddhism must have included the practice of meditation, which was the very essence of Ch'an. Meditation, with its emphasis on concentration, seems certainly to have aided Yang in developing his natural sensitivity to the passing moment and its ephemeral events. In poem after poem, Yang is concerned with transiency. He observes subtle alterations in the form and color of cloud transformations; he is fascinated by the effects of light and mist, by anything that may shift or change in an instant. The following three short passages are good illustrations of Yang's obsession with capturing the momentary changes in natural phenomena:

> The sunlight must be moving the waves by itself;
> the sky is calm, and there is no wind.

> With each passing moment, the clouds change color—
> now yellow, now purple, now deep blue-green.
> I sit and watch the clouds
>   floating in the blue sky:
> they turn into a dragon, its silver scales
>   clashing like cymbals.
> A moment later, the clouds fill the sky
> and only the scales are visible:
>   the dragon's body has disappeared.

Sometimes the transformation that takes place is unexpected to the point of being fantastic, as in "Passing by Hsin-k'ai Lake":

The fisherman poles his boat across the lake.
My old eyes watch him closely,
        until he does something strange:
he turns into a wild goose, standing on a reed.

Yang's genius for careful observation led him to compose an entire poem on the tiny movements of a fly:

      I see a fly
      warming himself on the windowsill,
      rubbing his legs, enjoying the morning sun.
      He seems to know when the light will shift:
      a sudden buzz
      and he's at another window.

It may have been Yang's skill at the detailed depiction of nature which inspired the poet Fang Yüeh (1199-1262) to dream that Yang was a painter. Fang describes his dream thus: "I dreamed that Lu Yu wrote out the words 'Joy of Poverty Studio' on a plaque for me, and that Yang Wan-li agreed to paint the studio walls. Actually, I have no such studio, nor did I know that Yang could paint." It was common for the walls of Chinese temples and studios to be adorned with landscape paintings, but, while Yang had a reputation as a calligrapher, there is no evidence that he ever painted.

Yang's most endearing quality is his humor. Often the final line of a *chüeh-chü* poem has the effect of a punch line: there is a delightful surprise, an unexpected leap of imagination for which the rest of the poem is a preparation. "Passing the Pavilion on Shen-chu Bridge" is such a poem:

      I get down from my palanquin
          and look around the country inn.
      I'm surprised by the cold sound of water beneath my feet.
      The Yangtze River is closer than I thought:
      suddenly, above the bamboo grove,
          an inch of mast floats by.

The appearance of the mast, on an infinitely smaller scale, is like the shock of enlightenment in Ch'an. Yang's wit or humor, however, is not always so subtle. In such poems as "Reading" (page 83) and "Don't Read Books!" (page 84), it can take on a gently self-mocking quality. Elsewhere, as in "To the Portrait Painter Wang Wen-shu" (page 105), it can become quite boisterous.

Yang wrote a number of remarkable poems dealing with fantastic, even visionary, themes. In these poems, Yang often appears as a skeptic whose doubts are dramatically rebutted by the powers of nature. In "A Visit to Yü's Cave" (page 98), for example, the speaker peers into the cave but wonders if the ancient sage-emperor could actually have stored his books in this place as legend had it:

> Yü lived so long ago;
> it's hard to tell if he was really here.

But at the end of the poem, when he looks back at the mountain, "The clouds are turning into dragons and tigers," as if to convince him that the spot really is possessed of magic power.

Similarly, in "Bamboo Hermitage" (page 99), Yang visits the site of the apotheosis of a famous Taoist immortal who rode to heaven on the back of a crane. Yang describes himself as "skeptical, suspecting a hoax, although he has donned the feathered robe of a Taoist adept. But after he inspects the "ancient egg" from which the crane was supposedly hatched, "Suddenly two old cranes swoop down from a pine tree with a long cry and perch on the eaves. " Yang takes this as an omen, a sign that his skepticism was mistaken:

> My heart skips a beat: I was wrong
> to doubt the power of this place.

The most extraordinary of Yang's poems in this mode is "Sudden Fog" (page 101). Yang may have been influenced by Ch'an Buddhism in his discussion of poetry and in his perception of the world, but "Sudden Fog" refers to a different kind of Buddhism, a popular, devotional religion in which the devotee can hope to experience visions of his favorite Buddha or *bodhisattva*. Certain mountains in China were associated with these apparitions, and Buddhists would make pilgrimages to them seeking visions or mystical experiences. In "Sudden Fog," Yang mentions one such site, Mount Omei in the western provence of Szechwan, particularly associated with the bodhisattva P'u-hsien, or Samantabhadra, to give his Sanskrit name. Yang's friend Fan Ch'eng-ta visited Mount Omei and described his journey in an essay entitled *A Trip to Mount Omei*, part of which throws interesting light on Yang's poem:

> "When Buddha is about to display a Great Manifestation, the cotton clouds spread out below the precipice, gather thickly, and rise to a point several tens of feet down. They then spread out like a smooth jade floor…. If one looks down from the precipice, one can see a great nimbus lying flat on the smooth clouds, surrounded by three halos, each white, yellow red and purple in color. In the center of the nimbus there is an area of congealed light—in this the observer can see his own form complete in every detail, as if in a mirror. If he raises his arms or moves his legs, the reflection will do the same. And he will not see the reflections of the people standing next to him. The monks call this the 'body-reflecting light.'
>
> "After this light has disappeared, windblown clouds arise from the mountain in front, and among them there appears a great nimbus-manifestation light arching across all the peaks, displaying a variety of colors which blend into beautiful patterns. At this time, the mountains and plants are all fresh and brilliant—it is impossible to look at them directly. Then the clouds and fog disperse, and the light remains. This is called a 'pure manifestation.' Ordinarily, when Buddha's light is about to appear, clouds spread out first. This is the so-called World of Cotton. The light-forms

emerge in the clouds. Those which do not depend on clouds are known as 'pure manifestations' and are very rare.

"After a moment, the light moves to the west of the mountain, and if you look to the left, toward the Mountain of the Thunder Cave Temple, another light, smaller than the previous one, can be seen. Before long it too flies beyond the mountain, where it turns until it is straight across the precipice. Then its color and form change, and it becomes a golden bridge that looks something like the Bridge of the Hovering Rainbow on the Wu River, with purple clouds supporting it on both sides. Most of the cloud forms disappear in the period between *tzu* and *wei* [11:00 A.M. to 3:00 P.M.]. But the golden bridge continues to be visible until the *yü* period [5:00 to 7:00 P.M.], and only then does it disappear."

Of particular interest is the golden bridge that appears both in Fan Ch'eng-ta's description of the apparitions at Mount Omei and in Yang's poems, and the fact that in describing the clouds both writers use the Chinese equivalent of the Sanskrit word for cotton, *tula*. Apparently, Yang had either been told of the Mount Omei phenomena or he had read Fan's account. His initial reaction was the usual skepticism: "I laughed at Buddha for deceiving the ignorant." But the personal experience described in the poem, like the clouds in "A Visit to Yü's Cave" and the cranes in "Bamboo Hermitage," suggest to Yang that his doubts may have been ill founded:

> Laugh at deception and be deceived—
> then Buddha will have the last laugh.

Buddha, manifested as the Mountain Spirit, teases Yang for his disbelief by unfolding before him the very visions which the poet had previously denied could exist.

There is a universality in certain visionary experiences, and so it may not be as extraordinary as it at first seems that an apparition nearly iden-

36

tical to Yang's is described by the modern American anthropologist Carlos Castaneda. Castaneda has become famous for his compelling books describing his experiences under the tutelage of an old Yaqui Indian whom he calls Don Juan. Initiated by Don Juan into the use of peyote and other hallucinogenic plants, Castaneda comes to realize that there is a "separate reality," another way of perceiving the world. Don Juan frequently sends him into the mountains of the Mexican desert to experience through isolation and concentration this special way of perceiving natural phenomena. During one such sojourn in the mountains, described in *Journey to Ixtlan* (New York: Simon and Schuster, 1972; pp. 156-57, 165-67), Castaneda sees "a bank of fog...which was descending from the top of the mountain." Don Juan asks him to focus his eyes on a "vague greenish area" in the fog without blinking. "And then," Castaneda writes, "I saw a thin strip of fog in between that looked like a thin, unsupported structure, a bridge joining the mountain above me and the bank of fog in front of me.... It was as if the bridge were actually solid.... I stared at the bridge, dumbfounded." But even though he sees the bridge, Castaneda stubbornly maintains later that it was not real. Don Juan asserts that the bridge was indeed real, but that Castaneda thinks "it is very helpful to keep on doubting and nagging." But Don Juan interprets the bridge as a manifestation of "power" which happened to take the form of a bridge. He cautions Castaneda that "the real battle will take place when you cross that bridge. What's on the other side? Only you will know that.... In order to journey through those unknown trails and bridges one must have enough power of one's own."

Castaneda's skepticism is reminiscent of Yang's. Like Yang, he is a visionary in spite of himself. The "power" which he unwittingly encounters is comparable to the Buddha-nature which manifests itself at Mount Omei, a "place of power" like the one to which Don Juan led Castaneda. And both men—the twelfth-century Chinese poet and the twentieth-century American anthropologist—see magical bridges appearing out of the fog. There can, of course, be no question of influence here. If a "rational" explanation is to be sought, it lies only in the realm of Jungian archetypal images.

Yang is often referred to as the *pai-hua shih jen* (colloquial poet) because the diction of his most characteristic poems has a natural flow resembling that of everyday spoken language, although kept within the strict confines of Chinese verse forms. Yang favored the use of colloquialisms in his poetry, believing, however, that these expressions should have precedents in the writings of earlier poets. The scholar Lo Ta-ching (fl. c. *1224*), who as a child heard Yang recite one of his poems, quotes Yang to this effect: "In poetry, it is certainly true that one sometimes transforms the vulgar into the refined, but such usages should undergo the influence of past poets—only then can they be used. Examples are *nai k'o* ['how can you?'] as used by Li Po, *che-mo* ['to such an extent'] as used by Tu Fu, and *li hsü* ['inside'] and *jo ke* ['which one?'] as used by the T'ang poets." It is quite possible that Yang was defending himself here against charges that he was vulgar in his diction, a condemnation often made by hostile critics during Yang's lifetime and in the centuries since.

Critical opinion on Yang's importance as a poet has always been sharply divided, but Yang has never been without admirers and defenders. His contemporary Chou Pi-ta (*1126–1204*), for example, praised Yang's work in an essay on the poem "A Trip to Stone Man Peak" (page *103*):

> "The long poems of Yang Wan-li seem to have been composed in the time it takes to walk seven steps, and yet not one word in them can be changed. His lines have power enough to command a thousand troops, drain the Three Gorges, pierce the center of heaven, penetrate the caves of the moon. He depicts the forms of things, and human feelings, in exhaustive detail, describing all their wonderful aspects.
>
> "Of course, such a man can be considered a born genius to whom writing comes naturally. But it must be kept in mind that from the age of fifteen until he was seventy, Yang modeled himself on the *Keng-tsai Song* [composed by the ancient sage-emperor Shun and his minister Kao Yao;

referred to in the classic *Book of Documents*], and carefully studied the poems of the *Book of Songs* [another classic work, compiled c. 600 B.C.], as well as the *Tso chuan* [a historical work], the *Chuang-tzu* [one of the Taoist classics], and the *Li sao* [an important ancient poem]. There was not one writer of the Ch'in [221-206 B.C.], Han [206 B.C.-A.D. 221], Chin [265-316], Southern and Northern dynasties [316-589], Sui [589-618], and T'ang [618-906] periods whose masterpieces he did not study, examining the origins of their diction and making selective use of their methods. For fifty years he practiced night and day, finally breaking through to a great enlightenment, so that the tip of his brush had a mouth, and his verses had eyes. How could this be achieved in a single day?

"I have seen Yang's long poem 'Stone Man Peak,' and reading it made me feel as if I were walking the twisting mountain path with my own feet and hearing the tiger with my own ears. I trembled inside, my hair stood on end. So greatly can poetry move us!"

Perhaps the most intelligent appraisal of Yang was made by the great Ch'ing-dynasty poet and critic, Yüan Mei (1716-98): "Someone compared Yüan's poetry with that of Yang Wan-li. Yuan said: 'Yang was one of the master poets of the Southern Sung. Later critics often made light of his poetry, but they didn't realize that he was a man of natural genius, like Li Po. It is true that he didn't polish certain flaws in his work, but this was the result of his honesty. I feel unworthy to be considered an imitator of his.'"

On the Relationship
of Poetry and Painting in China

Su Tung-p'o once said of Wang Wei, the great T'ang poet and painter: "There is poetry in his painting and painting in his poetry." This has become the standard dictum on the relationship of poetry and painting in China, a relationship that through the centuries has frequently concerned writers on both subjects.

In the West careful distinctions have long been drawn between the literary and the pictorial arts, whereas in China poetry and painting have been nearly inseparable and have been related to each other in a variety of ways. The Chinese poet and painter might well be one and the same person, Su Tung-p'o and Wang Wei being the two supreme examples of artist-writers as highly esteemed for their skills as painters as for their verse. In the West, such figures are rare. Michelangelo was a fine poet, but in neither the critical nor the popular mind does his writing equal his painting or his sculpture. Perhaps only William Blake corresponds well to the Chinese conception of the poet-painter, an artist using similar themes and images in both his poems and his paintings and even integrating poetry and painting in his illustrated books.

The practice of inscribing poems on paintings, or on special sections of paper attached to the paintings for just this purpose, was another aspect of the close relationship between poetry and painting. The poem might be written by the painter himself, by a friend of his, or by a later owner or connoisseur. Often, the poem includes images which do not appear in the painting, so that while the physical beauty of the picture is enhanced by the elegance of the calligraphy in which the poem is written, the imaginary world conjured up by the painting may be further expanded by the imagery of the poem. Sometimes the poem is the work of an earlier poet, but often it is an original poem by the artist himself. A perfect example is the hand scroll by the Yüan artist Wu Chen (1280-1354), reproduced on page 72, showing a fisherman seated in his boat gazing into the water. Wu has inscribed the following poem of his own composition in the upper right-hand corner of the picture:

> West of the village,
> evening rays linger on red leaves
> as the moon rises over yellow reeds on the sandbank.
> The fisherman moves his paddle, thinking of home—
> his pole, lying in its rack,
> will catch no more fish today.

The poem adds an image that is entirely absent from the painting—that of the village—and colors the leaves and reeds red and yellow, although in the picture they are done in shades of gray ink. We learn that it is sunset, and that the fisherman is thinking of returning home. Because these enhancements of the picture are expressed in words, they affect the viewer on a subtler level than the purely visual, and deepen his experience of the total work of art. Sometimes, when painter and poet are two different people, the picture will inspire the poet to reflect on his personal situation, as in the famous poem by Su Tung-p'o, inscribed on the painting *Misty River* and *Tiered Mountains* by a contemporary, the landscapist Wang Shen. After a long description of the scene, Su recalls his past happiness while living on the Yangtze River, and longs for the day when he will be able to return to nature (referring to himself as the Gentleman of the Eastern Slope):

> Saddening my heart, a thousand tiers of mountains along the
>   river
> shimmer with blue-green colors across the sky like clouds
>   or mist.
> Are they mountains? Are they clouds? It's hard to tell,
> but when mist opens and clouds disperse, the mountains
>   remain.
> Here I see two verdant cliffs, shadowing a deep valley,
> and a hundred cascades that fly down the cliffs,
> twist through forests, coil around rocks, hide and reappear,

then rush down to the valley mouth to form a stream.
The stream grows calm, the mountains open, and the foothill
forests end;
a tiny bridge and rustic shops lean against the mountain.
Travelers pass beyond the tall trees;
a fishing boat floats, light as a leaf.
The river swallows the sky.

Where did the governor find this painting,
its limpid beauties brushed by such a sensitive hand?
Where in our world is there such a place?
I'd go there now, and buy myself an acre or two of land!
But I remember an isolated spot at Fan-k'ou, near Wu-
ch'ang,
where the Gentleman of the Eastern Slope resided for five
years.
Spring breezes rippled the river; the sky was vast.
Summer rain clouds curled up at dusk; the mountain glowed.
Crows shook branches of red maple leaves before my river
home.
Winter snows, dropping from towering pines, woke me
from my drunken sleep.
The flowing waters of Peach Blossom Spring are in this
world;
why insist that the Wu-ling story was only a fairy tale?

But the rivers and mountains are fresh and pure,
while I am covered with dust;
there may be a path that leads to them, but it's hard to find.
With many a sigh, I return the scroll,
and wait for a friend who lives in these mountains
to send me a poem, "Come back!"

Although less frequent, the opposite phenomenon might also occur; that is, a painter might be inspired by a poem to do a picture based on the poem.

On a more profound level, Chinese poetry and painting are related in the fundamental similarity of their creative processes. Not only are the themes and images of both arts essentially conventional, or traditional, but those that appear in painting are the same as those used in poetry. For this reason, it is not surprising to find that a particular image—the fisherman, for instance, as an exemplar of Taoist freedom—will appear in a poem of the fourth century B. C., and again in a poem of the eighteenth century. Similarly, the same image of the fisherman will appear in a painting listed in a T'ang-dynasty catalogue and also in a picture by one of the Eight Eccentrics of Yang-chou, a group of Eighteenth-century artists.

In fact, the standard images of both poetry and painting were catalogued in two important encyclopedias, both published in the early eighteenth century. One, the famous *Chieh tzu yüan hua chuan* (The Mustard Seed Garden Manual of Painting), appeared in its final form in *1701*. This work is a collection of all the traditional images of Chinese painting, including mountains and rocks painted in various styles, trees and flowers of many kinds, birds and insects, temples, villas, and scholars and fishermen in boats. The other encyclopedia was the *P'ei-wen yün-fu* (The P'ei-wen Treasury of Rhymes), published in *1711*, but using material going back to the Yüan dynasty (*1279-1363*). This is a compendium of poetic images and phrases, each of which is quoted in chronologically arranged passages. Every image in *The Mustard Seed Garden Manual* can be found here as well. Under the heading "fisherman" (*yü-fu*), the passages quoted range from the earliest poem on this theme, found in the Ch'u tz'u anthology, much of which dates back to the fourth century B.C., to a Northern Sung poem by Su Tung-p'o—"I should meet the old fisherman here, / Winding his way through the reeds." The second line of Su's couplet is a quotation from a passage in the Taoist classic, the *Chuang-tzu*, also dating from the fourth century B.C., where Confucius meets a fisherman who "winds his way through the reeds." Clearly, the Chinese mind was accustomed to leaping easily over centuries.

Yang Wan-li was particularly fond of creating new variations on old themes. One of his versions of the fisherman theme is novel in that it removes the fisherman and leaves us with only the boat:

> It is a tiny fishing boat, light as a leaf;
> no voices are heard from the reed cabin.
> There is no one on board—no bamboo hat,
>   no raincoat, no fishing rod.
> The wind blows the boat, and the boat moves.

In a Western context, it would be unthinkable to illustrate a collection of Rimbaud's poetry with the paintings of, say, Ingres. Even though the two men lived in the same century, their styles and modes of expression are so very divergent that any attempt to link them seems foolhardy. But there is nothing incongruous in juxtaposing, as in this book, a poem by a twelfth-century Chinese writer with a picture by a painter of the seventeenth or eighteenth century; though widely separated in time, the two artists might well share the same vocabulary and much the same perception of life and nature.

A NOTE ON THE TRANSLATIONS

I have chosen to translate the poems of Yang Wan-li, called the colloquial poet by his contemporaries, into colloquial American English. Like most modern translators of Chinese poetry, I have not used rhyme, even though the original poems do rhyme in Chinese. The Chinese language is far richer in rhymes than English, and any attempt to capture all or most of the original rhymes in an English translation would inevitably seem forced and contrived.

With the exception of the two lyrics to the tune "Chao-chün's Sorrow" (page 74) and the lyric to the tune "Remembering the Girl of Ch'in" (page 75), which are in the *tz'u* form characterized by lines of uneven length forming set patterns, all the poems translated here are in the *shih* form. In this classic form of Chinese poetry, each line of a given poem consists of five or seven (very occasionally, six) monosyllabic characters.

The poems collected in this book are not arranged chronologically, but rather in a sequence suggested by theme or mood. The chronological order of the poems may be determined as explained in the note at the beginning of the Index of Titles and First Lines.

I have intentionally refrained from annotating the poems, except where a brief explanation seemed essential to conveying the meaning of a particular word or reference. My determination to avoid lengthy annotation is based first on the fact that Yang's poems are largely free of the abstruse literary allusions that make so many Chinese poets difficult to read without the aid of notes and extensive commentaries. Second, and even more importantly, I hope I have been successful in my effort to make the translations strong enough to stand on their own as poems in English.

ACKNOWLEDGMENTS

It would be impossible for me to thank individually all the many friends and scholars who have helped me in the writing of this book. I am deeply grateful to the teachers who introduced me to the world of classical Chinese literature and who have guided me with care and patience through the intricacies of reading, understanding, and translating Chinese poetry. Among them, I am particularly indebted to Hans Bielenstein, C. T. Hsia, and Burton Watson. Professor Watson's superb translations of Chinese poetry have set a high standard for any aspiring translator, and have had an invaluable influence upon my own work.

The proposal for a book of Yang Wan-li's poems originated with the Asian Literature Program of the Asia Society of New York, assisted by a grant from the National Endowment for the Humanities. Through the activities of the program, Bonnie Crown, Andrea Miller, and Zelda Bradburd have been untiring in their efforts to deepen the understanding and appreciation of Asian literature among readers in the West, and I am grateful for their constant encouragement and support.

The book is much enhanced by its illustrations, and I would like to thank Stephen Addiss for providing his excellent photographs of Chinese paintings that serve here to illuminate the poems of Yang Wan-li.

Finally, it is most difficult for me to express adequately my gratitude to the late John M. Crawford, Jr., whose generosity made possible the use of illustrations from his magnificent collection of Chinese art. His appreciation of the close relationship between poetry and painting in China and his concern for bringing before a Western audience something of the splendor of Chinese culture were major factors in the creation of this book. But beyond all else, his friendship and encouragement were a source of continuing inspiration.

HEAVEN MY BLANKET, EARTH MY PILLOW

Written on a Cold Evening

The poet must work with brush and paper,
but this is not what makes the poem.
A man doesn't go in search of a poem—
the poem comes in search of him.

Boating Through a Gorge

Here turtles and fish turn back,
and even the crabs are worried.
But for some reason poets risk their lives
to run these rapids and swirl past these rocks.

Taking the Ferry at Ta-kao

Fog veils the river and the mountains,
but sounds of dogs and chickens
            show that a village lies ahead.
The wooden planks of the ferry deck are covered with frost:
my boot makes the first footprint.

Going to Hsieh's Lake by Boat

1.

The wind blows toward the north,
        then it shifts to the south.
I blink—and we've traveled from the Yellow Fields
        to Hsieh's Lake.
The shadow of a mountain floats past my cabin;
I lift the curtain and see purple cliffs.

2.

I pour two cups of clear wine,
then open my cabin door.
Here are ten thousand wrinkled mountains
        that no one ever sees,
the highlights picked out for me by the setting sun.

Evening View From a Boat

We sail past a pine-tree forest on the river bank.
A man is walking where the trees end.
A mountain moves in front of the man, blocking our view.
The blue flag of a wine shop flutters in the wind.

To break the silence,
the boatman picks up his flute and plays into the mist...

Lying in the boat, stoned on wine, I take off my headcloth and chant poems...

STAYING OVERNIGHT AT HSIA-SHA STREAM

Trees, laced in mountain mist,
   patch broken clouds;
the wind scatters a rainstorm of fragrant petals.
The green willows, it is said, are without feeling—
why then do they try so hard to touch the traveler
   with their catkins?

PASSISNG THE LAKE OF THE FIGHTING PARROTS

Painted barges like mountains floating on the water;
small boats like ducks avoiding the shore;
red banners, green canopies, the clang of gongs—
people everywhere, saying hello or saying goodbye.

ON THE WAY TO T'UNG-LU

I sit napping in my palanquin
   as my cup of tea wears off.
There are no words on the milestones
   along these long mountain roads.
The crows and magpies jabber in a language I can't understand.
We pass a loquat tree; every leaf is yellow.

PASSING BY WATERWHEEL BAY

Reading in my palanquin, I fall asleep and dream—
dream of a fishing boat, lapped by waves....
When I awake the wind is riffling the pages of my book
and I can't even find the right chapter.

PASSING AN-JEN BY BOAT

Two little boys in a fishing boat—
they pull in their paddles and sit quietly.
Though it isn't raining, they hold up umbrellas,
not to cover their heads, but to catch the wind.

HAVING MY HAIR COMBED IN THE BOAT
ON MY WAY TO AN OFFICIAL POST

I ask my boy to comb my hair;
when I get past the itchiness
            each stroke feels so good,
                        better than fancy styling.
But nobody understands the most pleasant part of all—
closing my eyes,
            letting my head hang down
                        until I fall asleep.

Seventh Day of the First Month: Spring Scene at South Stream

I sit and watch the clouds
        floating in the blue sky:
they turn into a dragon, its silver scales
        clashing like cymbals.
A moment later, the clouds fill the sky,
and only the scales are visible:
        the dragon's body has disappeared.

Passing Yen-shih-pu by Boat

It is raining; the sail blocks our view.
We raise it, and the scene becomes even more beautiful.
Tall pines stand like writing brushes on the bank,
their cold reflections rippling into snakes.
Then a silver mirror floats out of the clouds,
and rays of morning light glitter on the jade sand.
We go to the bow and gaze into the distance
at range upon range of green mountains.

THE BOATMAN'S FLUTE

Today there is no wind on the Yangtze;
the water is calm and green
with no waves or ripples.
All around the boat
light floats in the air
over a thousand acres of smooth, lustrous jade.

One of the boatmen wants to break the silence.
High on wine, he picks up his flute
and plays into the mist.
The clear music rises to the sky—
   an ape in the mountains
   screaming at the moon;
   a creek rushing through a gully.
Someone accompanies on the sheepskin drum,
   his head held steady as a peak,
   his fingers beating like raindrops.

A fish breaks the crystal surface of the water
and leaps ten feet into the air.

IN THE GORGE: WE ENCOUNTER WIND

Our boat is becalmed in the middle of the river—
the mountains are silent and gloomy at sunset.
Suddenly a clap of thunder sounds in the darkening sky
and the trees along the shore begin to sway.
A powerful wind blows in from the southern sea
and sweeps angrily through the gorge.
The sailors cheer;
       the great drum is beaten.
One man flies to the top of the mainmast.
As the sail unfurls I pull my hands into my sleeves
and watch ripples like goose feathers
       swirl by in the water.

CROSSING TS'EN RIVER

Skinny rocks—verdigris green;
putrid water—bile yellow.
Here there are no hoofprints;
the twisting trail has run out.

Now the path starts again,
rougher than anything ever dreamed of.
Even with cold scraping our faces,
sweat pours from us like sauce.

CROSSING A BRIDGE

I stop halfway across the flimsy bridge;
the deep water frightens me.
I think of returning—but I'm halfway already.
I think of advancing—but I'm too dizzy to move.
Finally, I make it—but still I look back,
wondering how deep the water was.
Won't anybody rebuild this bridge
so we travelers can feel more secure?

TRAVELING EARLY ON DRAGON STREAM

The mountains and streams are covered with thick vapors—
not mist, not fog, not cloud.
Fellow Northerners, if you have never seen these miasmas of
        the South,
come to Dragon Stream and I'll show them to you.

CROSSING JUN-P'O BRIDGE

I start to walk over Jun-p'o Bridge,
wondering when I will reach Chiang-tung.
Suddenly I notice a marker in the middle of the bridge
and realize that half of my foot is already there.

Walking Along the Seashore

As I walk along the seashore the path becomes sandy;
the ocean wind blows up a sandstorm like thick fog.
I close my eyes, afraid to keep them open;
walking becomes harder with each step.
Step after step, my sandals sink deeper;
I'm moving my feet, but I'm getting nowhere.
Will I ever come to a place where there isn't any sand?
I'd rather scratch my toes on sharp rocks,
or get mud all over my clothes.
I don't want to walk on sand anymore.

Fourth Day of the Fourth Month:
I Cross the Border Between Che-tung and Yung-feng

A thousand peaks converge above me;
I walk a straight road through them.

The sunlight must be moving the waves by itself;
the sky is calm, and there is no wind.

I hold a cup brimming with village wine.
Red flowers hang limp at noon.

I guess I never fooled the milestones;
they reprimand me for ever going east.

This poem was written in 1179, while Yang was returning westward to his home after leaving his position. The milestones seem to "reprimand" him for having left home to become an official.

59

PASSING THE PAVILION ON SHEN-CHU BRIDGE

I get down from my palanquin
            and look around the country inn.
I'm surprised by the cold sound of water beneath my feet.
The Yangtze River is closer than I thought:
suddenly, above the bamboo grove,
            an inch of mast floats by.

STAYING OVERNIGHT AT WILLOW BANK INN

When are my travels ever going to end?
My old body has come to this inn again.
The roadside pines and junipers are ten years older,
once short, but now tall and stately.
The place where I stopped last night is far away;
and tomorrow, tonight will be last night.
In just an instant the present has become the past—
I'd have to be a saint not to drink wine!

PASSING SOUTH STREAM BRIDGE ON THE WAY HOME

One blast of cold wind,
and the clouds part above the mountains.
It is evening:
            the woodcutters' songs become even sadder.
The boy calls to his friends on the other bank;
they come to him, riding a water buffalo across
            the stream.

RED PEONIES IN A VASE

Afraid that the autumn wind
            might be jealous of the peonies,
I cut a branch and put it
            in a porcelain vase.
The heavy curtains are drawn,
            the doors are closed—
why do the petals keep falling off?

CHILLY

I stuff the heater with wood,
        and put on all my clothes—
but only drinking a cup of wine
        makes me really warm.
People say the cold is unbearable after frost,
but they don't realize that there's springtime
        in the wine pot.

DRINKING AT NIGHT

I drink alone in my cold study,
huddled close to the brazier.
The wine is fresh—just strained this evening.
The candle is short—left over from last night.
I chew on a piece of sugar cane as big as a rafter
and eat tangerines sweeter than honey.
When the wine takes effect, a poem comes to me;
I grope for my brush, but I'm too high to write it down.

Eating Frost to Sober Up

Hung over from last night's wine—
my chest is heavy, my stomach upset.
Below the railing on Peony Bank
I break off a ball of frost
              and roll it down my tongue.

In the Canal Locks at Hung-tse

Blocking the canal locks are cakes of ice
waiting for the people to open the gates.
When the gates are opened just two or three turns
the ice rushes through with a sound like splitting jade.

APPROACHING FOXGLOVE RAPIDS

Three and a half miles from Foxglove Rapids,
and already we hear the distant roar of the water.
Our mast begins to shake
as if afraid of the approaching struggle.
The boatmen steady their poles
ready to do battle with the enemy.
We raise the sail for a better view
and see whitecaps dashing against the rocks.
But as we approach we see it is only a waterwheel
singing a prelude to the rapids ahead.
Who knows what the real rapids will be like?
Maybe we were frightened for nothing.

RUNNING THE TS'AO RAPIDS

Lying in the boat, stoned on wine,
I take off my headcloth and chant poems.
We are running the rapids,
            but I'm too high to worry....
When we've made it I look back
            at the boats behind us
and realize what we've been through.

PASSING STONEBANK

The narrow stream twists and turns
          through thousands of rocks;
our little boat changes direction
          a hundred times.
All of us laugh
          while we're shooting the rapids.
When we've left them behind
          we start to feel depressed.

PRYAING FOR RAIN AT NIGHT IN THE LAO-KANG TEMPLE

There's never been such a hot autumn before:
tonight the moon is out, and it still isn't cool.
The withered sprouts are angry with me:
          "You lazy poet !"they seem to say,
"why don't you write a poem praying for rain?"

Watching Fish

Unable to take the heat,
I sit barefoot on a clay cushion
watching the fish in the pond.
I gaze at them, counting them again and again—
but I seem to frighten them;
they're afraid to swim across the pond.
Finally, one fish swims ahead
as if to show the others there is nothing to fear.
They start to follow him
but quickly lose their courage and turn back.

I drink cup after cup of wine....
Suddenly the sun is at the horizon.

Drinking Alone Beneath the Moon on a Summer Night

Who says this is a hot year?
Tonight it's unusually cool.
The breeze in the bamboo grove
             turns summer into autumn;
the moon, reflected in the stream,
             turns night into day.
Heaven rarely grants us such weather.
Though I'm alone, I pour a cup of wine.
Tomorrow the fiery umbrella will be in the sky,
and I'll have to think of some way
             to escape the heat.

Early Summer: Drinking Wine in a Boat

Wine is bad for me in the heat of early summer:
it overheats me and I can't fall asleep.
I prefer to let other people do the drinking
while I get high just watching them.
They drink, and I swallow—
because what I like in wine goes beyond the taste.

My fellow travelers think I'm crazy
but I don't want to get drunk like them.
Who knows the difference between high and sober anyway?
what it means to be really high?

Shadows on the Eastern Window

No need to paint a picture of sparrows and plum blossoms:
the sun has shadowed them against the paper window.
The sparrows can fly and the flowers can dance—
such a picture has never been painted before.

On a Painting of a Mounted Archer by Li Kung-lin

The warrior, brave as a tiger,
        gallops past the Western Palace
and pierces the target ball with a single arrow.
This picture of a mounted archer
        must have been painted in heaven—
Kung-lin stole it and brought it down
        to the human world.

*Li Kung-lin (c. 1040-1106) was one of the great figure painters
of the Northern Sung dynasty.*

Napping in a Boat

My mind is sluggish at noon; I don't want to stay up.
So I lie down on a bamboo pillow and try to fall asleep.
Everything gets hazy—I don't know if I am dreaming or awake.
I hear human voices, and the sound of the river.

PASSING BY HSIN-K'AI LAKE

The fisherman poles his boat across the lake.
My old eyes watch him closely,
        until he does something strange:
he turns into a wild goose, standing on a reed.

THE FISHING BOAT

It is a tiny fishing boat, light as a leaf;
no voices are heard from the reed cabin.
There is no one on board—
        no bamboo hat,
            no raincoat,
                no fishing rod.
The wind blows the boat, and the boat moves.

EVENING LAKE SCENES

1.

The lake seems glued to the sky—
          no banks are visible.
In the middle of the lake, water plants float.
It is evening—geese are forming V's,
          crows are forming flocks;
they land, then fly up again,
          taking a long time to settle for the night.

2.

I sit watching the sun set over the lake.
The sun is not swallowed by mountains or clouds:
it descends inch by inch, then disappears completely,
leaving no trace where it sinks into the water.

CLEARING AFTER RAIN

Where rain strikes the mountain the clouds begin to open;
the young rice sprouts are touched by faint sunlight.
Two blackbirds chatter in a flowering tree.
They look around, see nobody, and fly to the ground.

One fish swims ahead as if to show the others there is nothing to fear...

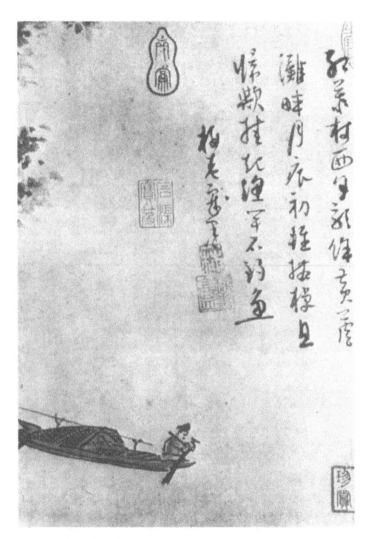

I watch the sun descend inch by inch, leaving no trace where it sinks in the water...

Walking in the Office Garden on a Warm Spring Day

Everywhere the spring birds are singing their new songs
and delicate flowers celebrate the soft air.
I explore each corner of the winding path,
making sure not to waste a single step.

Looking at Yüeh-t'ai Mountain From the Lien-t'ien Pavilion

At sunset the green mountain is pale one moment,
        dark the next,
brushed by layers of floating mist.
Thousands of cloud scrolls enfold the peak
in a screen of red brocade.

Two Lyrics to the Tune "Chao-chün's Sorrow"

1.

Yesterday evening I was drinking in my study when a gull perched
on the tip of one of the pine trees. A while later he flew away.
I was moved to write this poem.

I hear wings flapping in the pine tree
         and know that a gull has perched there.
I tell my son not to shout
and scare him away.
Suddenly, he flies off,
flies to some unknown place.
"I've quit my job!"
I yell after him.

2.

At noon I dream that I'm lying in a boat under some flowers;
fragrant mist covers West Lake.
Then the sound of rain
beating against the sail
wakes me from my dream.
It is rain falling on the lotus leaves:
the drops scatter like pearls,
then flow together like a pool of mercury
and roll off into the waves.

TO THE TUNE "REMEMBERING THE GIRL OF CH'IN": EARLY SPRING

Spring is early this year—
it is here ten days before spring should come.
Before spring should come—
falling plum blossoms like snow;
little red petals of wild peach.

The old man doesn't care
        that the new spring makes him older.
His only plan is to get good and drunk
        and fall down among the flowers.
Fall down among the flowers—
the boy supports him, takes him home.
When he sobers up the window is filled with morning light.

THE TWIN PAGODAS OF ORCHID STREAM

The tall pagoda is not pointed, the short one is.
One of them wears an embroidered robe,
the other a silver skirt.
Do you wonder why they never say a word?
It's because the rapids speak for them
with the voice of Buddha.

I Visited the Cloud Edge Temple
But the Monks Had All Gone Out, So I Went on to a Farm

Evening approaches—
I have climbed each mountain and I am tired.
In search of a pot of tea
I go to a local temple.
It is deserted.
There is not one monk left.
On the way home I stop at a farmer's house
          to spend the night.

I Planned to Stay Overnight at P'ing-hsiang
But Some Important Guests Were Occupying the Inn There,
So I Had to Go Out to the Western Suburbs

Chanting poems, I lose track of the rise and fall of the road.
Suddenly I'm startled to see the tips of pine trees at my feet.
I was planning to get drunk and sleep at P'ing-shih station;
now I must go further west,
          west of the station,
                    west of the mountain.

Who says that poets love the mountains?
Mountains, mountains—
        I'm tired of writing about them!
Thousands of peaks and thousands of ranges
        seem to throw themselves at me.
I have to rest three hours for each hour of climbing.

When your desk is piled high,
        where can you put another book?
When your stomach is full,
        how can you go on eating?
I have no use for more green slopes
        and mountain mists—
I'll wrap them in a package
        and send them to my city friends.

AFTER IT STOPPED SNOWING THE EVENING SKY CLEARED UP

In search of beautiful sights
        I forget the cold
and stand in the spring wind at sunset.
After the snow, under a clear sky,
        the eastern mountains are most beautiful—
silver peaks like waves in a soft red light.

The Cold Fly

I see a fly
warming himself on the windowsill,
rubbing his legs, enjoying the morning sun.
He seems to know when the light, will shift:
a sudden buzz
and he's at another window.

Laughing at a Bee

Herbs are baking in the brazier;
attracted by their fragrance,
           a bee buzzes around the room.
Do you know why the old man laughs out loud?
Because the bee depends on its nose to look for flowers.

WRITTEN AT THE CHENG FAMILY SHOP
ON THE DAY AFTER THE FIRST DAY OF SPRING

Stone cliffs and clumps of bamboo,
river pavilions and small towers—
the sound of the rapids clarifies the traveler's dreams;
in the shadow of the lamp the poet's sadness grows.

The first day of spring has vanished,
and soon the full-moon festival will pass.

What is making me unhappy,
making me knit my brow like this?

WATCHING THE MOON FROM THE FISHING BOAT
IN THE SNOW ON A FROSTY NIGHT

I stand by the stream waiting for the moon to rise,
but the moon knows my impatience and takes its time.
Tired of waiting, I go home and close the door;
suddenly the moon comes flying up over a thousand peaks.
So I climb to the Fishing Boat in the Snow and gaze
at the icy wheel hanging from the pine tips.

"As a rule, poets prefer the mid-autumn moon,"
someone says, but I shake my head:
"The twelfth month is the month for the moon,
when it's washed by snowflakes and scoured by frost.
Ten thousand miles of deep blue sky, like a pond
with a plate of white jade floating across it.
And then there are the plum blossoms....
Mid-autumn has none of these things."

"The Fishing Boat in the Snow" was the name of Yang's studio.

PLAYING WITH ICE

My son takes a piece of ice
            and hangs it from a colored thread
as if it were a silver gong.
He strikes it—the sound of jade chimes
            ringing through the forest;
then the sound of glass
            shattering on the floor.

Climbing the Pavilion of Pure Distance

I come through the snow
        to climb the Pavilion of Pure Distance.
Flying flowers alight on the river and turn to ice.
There are ten thousand acres of jade fields,
        a thousand pearl-strung trees.
I am truly twelve stories high on Jasper Terrace.

The Han-hsu Pavilion of Water Moon Temple

A slanting path leads to the temple gate.
Mist curls around my face and body.
Low roofs nestle among low trees.
Tiny flowers grow in miniature gardens.

Browsing through the library, I read Buddhist hymns
and catch glimpses of streets beyond the bamboo grove.
The friendly monks know that I am thirsty:
they get up to say hello and boil some tea.

Tai-tu Temple

I was here once before, fifteen years ago.
I recognize half the monks—the temple is the same.
In those days the willows were just starting to grow.
Now they rise beautifully above the high eaves.

The Pavilion Behind the Temple

Having visited all the empty rooms,
I come to a painted balustrade;
the glow of moonlit bamboo fills the cold pavilion.
A poem is inscribed on the wall,
and I wonder who wrote it.
High on wine, I hold up my candle,
and look closely at the words.

READING

When I read, I work hard at it,
but that makes me tired and dizzy;
so I put my book down and meditate—
then the book and I both forget about words.

When I feel like it, I flip the book open—
suddenly I've come to the Source of the Sages:
if I say this is enlightenment—
            basically there is no enlightenment;
if I say this is the Mystery—
            there has never been a Mystery.
It's just a moment of happiness
when I find a passage in harmony with my mind.
But who creates this happiness?
It isn't me, and it isn't Nature....

What a laugh! All my theories are wrong!
I throw the book down beside my pillow.

TO TSENG, THE FORTUNETELLER

You've thrown away all your scholarly books;
now you read books on fortunetelling
and look at scholars with cold eyes.
Master Tseng, will you be my friend?
Together we'll get into a fishing boat
and sail off to the Five Lakes.

Don't Read Books!

Don't read books!
Don't chant poems!
When you read books your eyeballs wither away,
        leaving the bare sockets.
When you chant poems your heart leaks out slowly
        with each word.
People say reading books is enjoyable.
People say chanting poems is fun.
But if your lips constantly make a sound
        like an insect chirping in autumn,
you will only turn into a haggard old man.
And even if you don't turn into a haggard old man,
it's annoying for others to have to hear you.

It's so much better
        to close your eyes, sit in your study,
        lower the curtains, sweep the floor,
        burn incense.
It's beautiful to listen to the wind,
        listen to the rain,
take a walk when you feel energetic,
and when you're tired go to sleep.

1.

I don't feel like reading another book,
and I'm tired of poetry—that's not what I want to do.
But my mind is restless, unsettled—
I'll try counting raindrop stains
        on the oilcloth window.

2.

I finish chanting my new poems
        and fall asleep—
I am a butterfly journeying to the eight corners
        of the universe.
Outside the boat, waves crash like thunder,
but it is silent in the world of sleep.

ON LIU TE-FU'S PAVILION OF REALITY

T'ao Ch'ien forgot words
        when he experienced reality.
Today his experience is still alive in your pavilion.
If a guest should ask you "What is this 'reality'?"
say: "A person's image in a mirror,
        the sky reflected in water."

Banana Leaves

When banana leaves are rained on they are happy:
all night long they sing in fresh, graceful tones—
the soft notes imitate flies
        rustling against paper;
the loud notes ring out
        like mountains spilling waterfalls.
Three drops, five drops—each distinctly heard;
there are no other sounds in the quiet autumn night.

The banana leaves are happy,
        but the poet is depressed:
he wants the west wind to stop,
        and the rain to stop.

Listening to Rain

A year ago my boat, homeward bound,
        moored at Yen-ling—
I was kept awake all night by the rain
        beating against the sails.
Last night the rain fell on the thatched roof
        of my house.
I dreamed of the sound of rain
        beating against the sails.

Ch'ing-yuan Gorge

In the morning there is heavy fog and rain.
I'm afraid to open the cabin door.
When I try to raise the window just a crack
the vapors rush in and fill the boat.
Without burning any incense
I am surrounded by fragrant mist.
My body is floating in the clouds, over the river—
there is not one speck of dust, anywhere.

Noon on the Day of the Autumn Moon Festival

After the rain the red sun beats down again;
high noon, and there is no shade.
The bees can find no flowers—
          their food supply is gone.
The ants try to make it home,
          but water blocks their way.

Today is supposed to be the autumn-moon festival,
but the weather is hotter than in midsummer.
I have come to the garden in search of coolness
          but there is only heat.
Sitting quietly, I burn incense and read T'ang poems.

Drinking Alone Beneath the Moon
on the Eleventh Night of the Seventh Month

This year the autumn sun is burning us to death,
but tonight the autumn moon beckons us to rise.
The moonlight is like water, cleansing my body;
the moon's color is like frost, cooling my bones.
I'm an old man who fears the heat as he would a tiger;
all my life I've loved the moon as if it were a jar of ice.
The moon should be seen with friends and not alone;
wine should be drunk and not refused.
So I call the jade rabbit and the golden toad
to share a cup of wine and some boïled vegetables.
Tomorrow morning the autumn sun will burn again,
but tonight I enjoy myself in the autumn moonlight
as the stars of Ts'an appear and the moon descends.

In Chinese folklore the jade rabbit and the golden toad both live in the moon.
Ts'an is the Chinese name for the constellation Orion.

Passing Ch'en's Trail

Once, passing Ch'en's Trail in a boat,
I raised my head to listen to the wind in the pines.
Now, a year later, I am standing in that wind
looking down at the boats traveling east and west.

EVENING: SITTING IN THE WO-CHIH STUDIO

The room is stuffy and uncomfortable:
I open a window to let in the cool air.
Forest trees shade the sunlight;
the inkstone on my desk glitters jade green.
My hand reaches naturally for a book of poetry
and I read some poems out loud.

The ancients had a mountain of sorrows
but my heart is as calm as a river.
If I am different from them,
how is it that they move me so deeply?

The feeling passes and I laugh to myself.
Outside a cicada urges on the sunset.

SLEEP

Only a little high, as if I had drunk no wine at all—
the chilly night seems to last a year.
I woke up at midnight and wrote down a dream
but couldn't go back to sleep.

Thousands of things rise from the depths of my mind
and appear before my eyes.
This lucid depression is unbearable—
a single wild goose crying in the cold sky.

SICK AND RESTLESS AT NIGHT,
I GET UP AND WALK IN THE MOONLIGHT

1.

I don't ask to be one of the three ministers;
there's enough to eat—who needs a lot of money?
I just want to lead a happy life
enjoying the moon and the wind.

2.

The summer days are hot, but tonight it is cool,
even cooler at two than it was at midnight.
Dew drips from the whiskers of the jade rabbit;
winds rise from the waves of the Milky Way.

The three ministers were the highest officials in the Chinese government.
The jade rabbit lives in the moon.

The twelfth month, when the mooon is washed by snowflakes and scoured by frost...

A gate that is never locked, and a simple roof,
just a handful of thatch, to keep out the frost and hail...

SITTING AT NIGHT ON THE MOON VIEWING TERRACE

This autumn the days have been hot
but each evening cool weather returns.
The last few nights I have sat outside
until the water clock struck the third watch.

Brisk wind, stars glittering and fading;
floating clouds, welcomed and seen off by the moon.
When I pursue happiness I can never find it;
now happiness has come of itself.

The Chinese divided the night into five watches of two hours each.
The third watch corresponded to the hours between 11:00 P.M. and 1:00 A.M.

RISING EARLY

Chrysanthemums in bloom—as gaunt as ever;
peonies, leaves falling off, seem completely withered.
A locust, frozen nearly to death,
clings desperately to a cold branch.

Reading in the To-chia Pavilion on a Clear Morning

Already a year has gone by
since I became governor of Ching-ch'i.
I can't complain about my office and residence,
but for some reason I've rarely been happy here.
If my servants aren't sick,
my children are crying.
We were once poor and didn't have enough to eat,
but it isn't hunger that's bothering me now.

Early in the morning I put a book in my sleeve
and climb to the pavilion to do some reading.
The moon and stars are still shining;
there is dew on the ground,
no shutters keep out the wind.
Suddenly I feel my old, sick body
can't bear clothing any more.
How did I ever get through the recent heat?
The cold is what I really like!
White birds look like butterflies in the distance;
a cicada hums what sounds like a poem.
The pine trees turn my spirit to snow;
I breathe in the icy fragrance of lotus.
In an instant sadness and happiness
have disappeared
and I feel as if I've left my body.

The children don't realize what's happening:
they call me down to eat breakfast.

The Tower of Flowing Blue-Green
Built by Liu Tao-hsieh of An-fu

South of the study, mountains encircle the buildings
like ten thousand hatpins of sliced jade.
North of the study, there are more mountains,
ten thousand waves in an emerald sea.
Here, Master Liu has built his tower,
with mountains to the south and to the north.
Intoxicated, he leads his guests to the very top,
and we are amazed to see blue-green waves flowing over dry
      land.

One wave surges above the clouds, halfway to heaven;
other waves splash the sky and moisten the Milky Way.
With a roar, the peaks rush toward the railing—
heaven jumps, earth leaps—the world has gone mad!

Host and guests clap their hands and call for a fishing boat.
But when we look again with sober eyes
all we see are mountains to the south and to the north.

DRINKING AT NIGHT IN THE BAMBOO PAVILION OF CHAO TUN-LI
IN YUNG-CHOU, WE HEAR THE DRUNKEN SINGING OF THE FROGS

We meet at night in the Thatched Pavilion
          and look down at ten thousand bamboos.
The early moon is pale, outshone by the tall candles.
Our host keeps urging us to drink, and soon, in a daze,
we have fallen to the Land of Intoxication.

Suddenly, in the grass, we hear the croaking of frogs;
they seem to laugh at us for drinking so little.
Their singing is beautiful frog music:
why insist that it should sound like flutes and drums?

I remember when we climbed together
          to the Pavilion of Ten Thousand Stones,
how we leaned on the balustrade, hands dangling,
          gazing at the cold, green bamboo.
Now we are actually in the cold green—
the bamboo will be unhappy
          if we don't drink some more.

The Cloud Nest of Tseng Wu-i

Master Tseng of Orchid Stream
ate orchids every day and drank water from the stream.
But his lotus-leaf robe was getting dusty,
so he moved far to the west, west of Dragon Mountain.

One clear morning he put on straw sandals
        and climbed to the mountain top;
there he saw a shred of cloud emerging from a rock.
Quickly he grabbed the cloud like a ball of cotton
and stuffed it in his shirt so it couldn't get away.
But a moment later the cloud escaped,
expanded, and filled the clear sky.
Then the Cloud God began to tease Master Tseng,
spreading out the cloud like a huge curtain,
        drawing it together like a robe.
He took Master Tseng by the hand and led him to the Cloud
        Nest,
where there was no sky above and no earth below.
Suddenly, the Thunder Goddess cried out;
astonished, Master Tseng saw that the cloud nest had
        disappeared.
So he went home and built a nest of his own;
and every night the clouds came there to rest.

A Visit to Yü's Cave

Once I rode a phoenix over the Nine Doubtful Mountains;
now I ride the wind up Mount Kuei-chi.
Yü's Cave is dark and deep—I peer down,
but Yü lived so long ago
it's hard to tell if he was really here.

Thin mists obscure the highest peaks.
A fine drizzle lightens the autumn heat.
When I look back toward the pine trees on the slope
the clouds are turning into dragons and tigers.

The setting of this poem is Mount Kuei-chi in Chekiang Province.
Yü the Great, a legendary hero who saved China from disastrous floods,
is said to have stored books in a cave on the mountain. Yü died and was buried at Kuei-chi.

Old men speak of Li the Immortal,
who once ascended to the outer limits of space.
He took along no unnecessary baggage,
only the crane he was riding on.
Cranes are not womb-born—they are hatched;
the shell of the ancient egg can still be seen today.
For a thousand years it has survived, as hard as stone,
sheltered at the foot of Phoenix Mountain.
On cold nights, in dark rain storms,
its magic light illuminates cliff and gully.
Dogs bark when they see it; cocks crow at night.
Dragons weep, frightening people in their beds.

Today the place is marked by Bamboo Hermitage,
a natural structure not formed by human skill.
On the very spot where the crane hatched from the egg
there is a gate that is never locked;
and a simple roof, just a handful of thatch,
keeps out the frost and hail.
Seen from far away, it resembles an old fisherman
wearing a raincoat of layered bamboo.

I have come to explore this hidden site,
still skeptical, suspecting a hoax.
I wear a feathered robe through the fog,
take off my sandals below the stone steps.
Entering the doorway, I walk around—
my voice echoes from inside the hollow egg.
The baby crane is long since gone,
but a snow-white membrane is still visible.

Suddenly, two old cranes swoop down from a pine tree
          with a long cry
and perch on the eaves.
My heart skips a beat: I was wrong
to doubt the power of this place.

Setting out at dawn, I gaze at the distant mountains;
I can count the peaks in the clear air.
But the budding hope in my heart
arouses the jealousy of the Mountain Spirit.
Swiftly he exhibits his divine powers
in a startling display of transformation.
He fills the air with cotton clouds
then tears them into shreds of silken mist.
They enfold the earth everywhere
and hide the sky from view.
The sun, like a plate of rose quartz,
hangs at a height beyond calculation—
it shines down through the haze,
red beams penetrating the white fog.
In the fog are human forms
coming and going in great confusion.
Each of them is holding some implement
but I cannot see clearly what they are.
Next, as if this weren't strange enough,
there appear even stranger sights:
a roadway lined with pearl-studded banners;
mountains covered with trees of jasper.
A golden bridge arching across the sky;
a jade pagoda surging up from the earth.
But while I stare in astonishment
everything is suddenly swept away.
Amazed, I rub my eyes,
and find myself standing on the same old mountain road.
Who can say if this was fantasy or reality,
whether I was dreaming or awake?
Once I traveled to Mount Omei in my imagination
and laughed at Buddha for deceiving the ignorant.

Laugh at deception and be deceived—
then Buddha will have the last laugh.

Mount Omei was a holy place for Buddhist devotees. Yang may have been familiar with the essay A Trip to Mount Omei, by his friend the poet Fan Ch'en-a-ta. With great descriptive power, Fan writes of various mysterious phenomena that are remarkably similar to those in Yang's poem. Among them are the "cotton clouds" (both Fan and Yang use the Chinese transliteration of the Sanskrit tula, "cotton"), and the golden bridge. Apparently Yang's poem combines memories of Fan's account with an actual personal experience.

HUI MOUNTAIN

If you look back at Hui Mountain from P'an-feng, it really has the shape of a dragon. The dragon has a Buddhist temple for a nose, and in front of the temple there is a small, smoothly rounded peak like a pearl. The tail of the mountain winds back forcefully, with a thick base and a tapered end.

Hui Mountain moves like a living dragon
with jade backbone and jasper waist.
He juggles a pearl above Monk's Staff Stream
as if playing with the moon beneath the waves of Lake T'ai.
Gray rocks are his horns, pine trees are his beard,
and the glittering gold in his beard is an old temple.
Look at the dragon from P'an-feng
and see his tail winding back below the pearl.

Two friends took a trip together to Stone Man Peak.
They walked far through green bamboo and yellow brush.
The narrow path made walking difficult;
halfway up the mountain, the path ran out.
When the friends started they could hear dogs barking from
        the villages,
but as they walked and as they talked, they got farther and
        farther away.
Soon there were no footholds above and no ledges below,
no way to climb on, no way to retreat.
Green bamboo and yellow brush, deeper and deeper
Suddenly, the notes of a flute sounded from the dark woods.
Below them in the grass was the body of a dead cow
and a pool of blood moistening the ground.
The two men looked at each other, their faces drained of
        color,
and then ran around the mountain to a temple.
When the monks heard their story they cried out in fear,
kicking over meditation benches and falling against the walls.
"How could you have heard a flute on this desolate mountain?
It was the breath of a crouching tiger!"

The friends came home and told me their story.
They said it was a fantastic trip.
Yes, it must have been fantastic indeed:
their lives were worth a handful of sand.

The master lived on tea; he ate no meat.
The master drank spring water; he never touched wine.
He put up with cold and hunger for seventy years,
but his fame shall endure for thousands of generations.

Hui Spring was renamed the Spring of Master Lu,
and now the spring and Master Lu are always named together.
A stick of Buddhist incense burns before his image;
crowds of monks bow down before the immortal of Tea.

The painted worthies of Unicorn Hall are fading in the cold;
the caps and swords of Ling-yen Pavilion have vanished like
        melting snow.
But Hui Mountain will turn to dust
and Hui Spring run out of water
before the Temple of Master Lu disappears.

Above the mountain, reflected in the spring:
        the wheel of the moon.

Lu Yü (d. 804) was the T'ang-dynasty author of the Classic of Tea. *Unicorn Hall, containing the paintings of worthy officials, was built during the reign of Emperor Hsüan (r. 73-47 B. C.) of the Han dynasty. Ling-yen Pavilion was a similarly decorated structure, built in 643 by Emperor T'ai-tsung of the T'ang dynasty.*

TO THE PORTRAIT PAINTER WANG WEN-SHU

I am not like a flourishing pine tree, thousands of feet tall.
I am not like the lustrous willow, growing in spring moonlight.
No, my wispy beard and thinning hair have turned to snow;
my creviced skin and wrinkled flesh are old and ugly.

When Master Yeh painted my portrait my face was still
        youthful.
But now, as Master Wang paints me, my bones are jutting out.
All my life I have written unconvincing poems about the
        mountains;
now my own shoulders have become a pair of skinny autumn
        peaks.

Don't you remember
that the Duke of Pao and the Duke of O
        were painted in Ling-yen Pavilion
with feathered arrows as big as pillars
        hanging at their waists?
And don't you remember the ink painting
        of the poet of Huan-hua Stream
drunk at sunset, riding a donkey, slipping in the mud?
Today, the noblemen and the poor scholar are equally
        laughable:
their portraits survive, but the men themselves have
        disappeared
Master Wang, Master Wang, please stop painting my portrait!
I'd rather drink a cup of wine while I'm still alive.

Ling-yen Pavilion, built in 643 by Emperor T'ai-tsung of the T'ang dynasty, contained portraits of worthy officials.

Master Liu Painted a Portrait of Me in My Old Age and Asked Me to Write a Poem About the Picture

Few hairs, made fewer by the comb;
short mustache, made shorter by the tweezers—
scratching my hair and twisting my mustache,
when will I ever stop looking for poems?

On a Portrait of Myself

The pure wind makes me chant poems.
The bright moon urges me to drink.
Intoxicated, I fall among the flowers,
heaven my blanket, earth my pillow.

A Visit From Wang Hsüan-tzu

As we've grown older we've had more and more troubles,
but how can we blame fate for our sadness?
In our lives we have been frustrated as writers
and entangled in official careers.

Bitter memories of sitting and talking together;
so hard to send off your boat after the snow!
We see each other once every three years—
and what is a lifetime divided by three?

Bubbles on the Water

The most precious treasure is never fully known.
The black dragon's pearl appears for an instant, then sinks
      again.
The jewel on the forehead of the Golden Buddha
is only half-visible to common men.

*The bubbles are compared to a legendary pearl, guarded by a black dragon, and to the urna,
the symbolic jewel at the center of the forehead of a Buddha image.*

A Visit to the Terrace of the King of Yüeh

I visit the old terrace
      above the tips of the banyan trees.
The ocean below looks like wine in a jade cup.
Here the King of Yüeh once sang and danced
      in the spring wind;
today there is only the spring wind.

THE PAGODA ON TURTLE MOUNTAIN

A pagoda stands on the highest peak of Turtle Mountain,
towering above the Huai River.
It is a silver brush doing calligraphy on the sky,
a jade dragon leaping from the earth,
          drawing waterfalls behind it.

Once the pagoda was attacked by a pack of wild dogs
but it resisted with the strength of ten thousand oxen.
Now the rebels' blood has petrified and turned to stone.
Only their ghosts remain, howling in the wind.

Wan-yen Liang, leader of the enemy Chin troops, once attempted to destroy the pagoda by having thousands of his soldiers pull on a huge silken cable which was tied to it. But the cable broke, and the pagoda remained standing. In 1161, Wan-yen Liang was defeated by the Chinese and was assassinated by one of his own men. The present poem was written in 1190.

READING BY THE WINDOW

I idly open a book of T'ang poems
and find a petal of peach blossom, still fresh.
I remember taking this book with me
          to read among the flowers
and realize that another year has passed.

Rainy Night: Unable to Sleep

A heavy rain starts to fall;
I can count the first few drops on the dry tiles.
The sound wakes me from my dreams
          of rivers and lakes;
I close my eyes, but cannot dream again.

The night is long, the wine I drank weak.
Sleep is sweet, the poet's thoughts bitter.

I cannot fall asleep.... I wonder
if I will ever sleep again.

A Sleepless Night

I hated the long winter nights,
          waiting for spring to come.
Now it is spring, and the night seems just as long.
I force my eyes closed, but can't fall asleep.
I rub my feet together, but they're still cold.
All night I listen to the wind in the pines
and watch my lantern burn dimmer and dimmer.
Finally I sit up and pull the blanket over my head,
casting the shadow of a sick monkey.

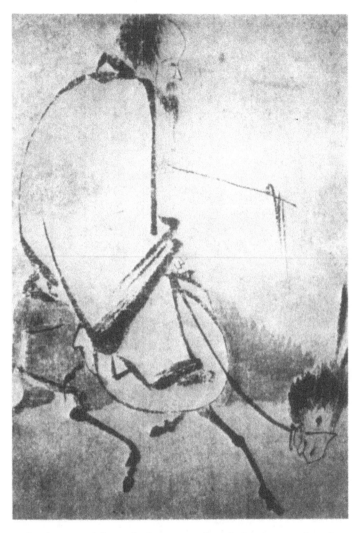

An ink painting of the poet drunk at sunset, riding a donkey, slipping in the mud...

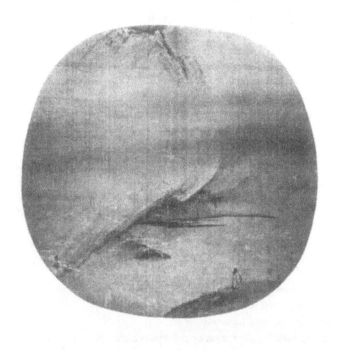

For the first time I understood the sound of spring rain on the river at night...

Late Spring: On the Way to Yung-ho

Not many days of spring are left
but living in the mountains, it's hard to tell:
green haze—wind blowing through the wheat;
white ripples—sunlight dancing on the pond.

The scene is beautiful, but I'm feeling bad;
everyone else is happy—I alone am depressed.
So I walk through the countryside, gazing around
and, when I feel like it, writing poems.

Sitting Up at Night in Late Spring

1.

Spring passes quickly—I am ill,
and spring looks like autumn to my sick eyes.
Only the dim lamp takes pity on me
and brightens my depression on a sleepless night.

2.

My pain cries to heaven,
        but heaven does not know.
Or heaven does know, but does not care.
I pick up the poems of Po Chü-i
and find a few moments of happiness.

THIRD DAY OF THE THIRD MONTH, RAIN:
WRITTEN TO DISPEL MY DEPRESSION

1.

I go out the door; it's raining, but I can't go back now,
so I borrow someone's bamboo hat to wear for a while.
Spring has tinted ten thousand leaves, and I didn't even know;
the clouds have taken a thousand mountains and swept them away.

2.

I look for flowers in the village
       but they hide from me on purpose;
and even when I find them, they only sadden me.
It would be better to lie down
       and listen to the rain
             in the spring mountains—
a quick downpour, then a few scattered drops.

3.

As spring dies the scenes grow more beautiful:
the poet will remember them for the rest of his life.
Level fields overflowing with green—
       wheat in every village;
soft waters reflecting red—
       flowers on every bank.

The Cold Lantern

Old and young, everyone's asleep.
The cold lantern, flickering at midnight,
       is my only companion.
The two flowers I've been looking at become dragonfly eyes;
the single flame, a jade vase hanging in the air.

Hearing Hsiao Po-ho and His Son Shang-ti Reading Aloud at Night

When I was young I was never away from my reading lamp;
I loved books so much that I grew thin and gaunt.
Now I'm old and lazy and can't read anymore;
instead, I lie and listen to my neighbors
       reading aloud at night.

Sick: Sitting Up at Night

The moon lingers in the Silver River;
it seems to yearn for the plum tree in the courtyard.
I hear the jade water clock drip out the second watch.
I snuff my candle and see the moon's halo.

Too ill to drink wine, I have to watch other people drink;
for some reason my sideburns are turning to snow.
Before long I'll become senile—will I ever regain my health?
Sixty-eight years old and starting to crumble.

I Recover From an Illness Only to Feel Old Age Coming On

When I was sick, it didn't bother me so much.
Now that I'm better, I'm starting to feel old.
But who can be strong and healthy forever?
Suddenly, old age will come.

The mountains are chilled by a cold sun.
Autumn light trickles into my poem.
A little pine tree sways in the wind
imitating the way I stroke my beard as I write.

Sunset

The spring breeze blows against my face,
        but doesn't sober me up;
my sick body feels the passing of the seasons.
The setting sun won't let me pretend
        that I'm not growing old:
its rays pick out two silver hairs in my mustache.

I finish my dinner
        and take a walk in the eastern garden,
                overwhelmed by depression.
Yesterday, when I was lying sick in bed,
I told myself I might never come here again.
Now, as I walk through the gate,
the wind starts to blow harder,
and the pine trees sing mournfully.
My sick body isn't up to this—
I should go back, but I can't help staying.
I stop in front of the southern studio
and rest on the moss-covered steps.
There aren't many flowers
only two flowering plum trees.
They must have known I was coming
and suddenly burst into bloom for me.
The bamboos also seem full of feeling;
they sway in the wind, striking strange poses.
I wonder if they are dancing happily
or if they are bending in fear of the wind?
All of nature seems to welcome spring;
I alone am old and sick.
Tomorrow will I be able to come again?
I'll go home now, and stir up the ashes in the fireplace.

In translating the last line, the alternate reading in the Ssu-pu ts'ung-k'an edition of this poem has been used: ch'ieh kuei po lu hui.

I Sit Lazily All Day Because My Feet Hurt

For three or four years
my eyes have been hazy,
   and my hair has turned to snow;
yet I've somehow managed to get along.
But now my feet hurt
   and I can't walk;
I stay home all day, sitting like a Zen monk!

I drop my fan beside the desk,
   but I'm too lazy to pick it up;
I try reading by the window,
   but I can't get anywhere.
People envy the immortals because they can fly;
for me, an immortal is a man who can walk.

Late Spring in the Capital: At the Inn of No Sorrows

My eyes are sick; I can't even open a book.
I decided not to receive visitors
   because of the spring mud
     but no one comes anyway.
Without any plans for passing the long day
I walk a hundred times around the railed terrace.

How can you stay awake all day?
At noon I think of taking a nap.
My bamboo bed has been warmed by the sun;
I toss and turn but cannot fall asleep.
So I get up, scratch my white head,
            and walk around the veranda a hundred times.

Just as I'm feeling most depressed
a strange thing happens to me—
a breeze blows through the northern door
and past the southern window,
            past the southern window,
                        wafting to me
the fragrance of young orchids.

Cooled by the breeze, this old man feels refreshed,
as if he had returned to life.
But in the future, at times like this,
will the breeze come again?

LIVING IN RETIREMENT:
AFTER A NAP ON AN EARLY SUMMER DAY

1.

In the shade of the pine tree, a trellis covered with moss;
I feel like reading my book, but I'm too lazy to open it.
Playfully I cup a handful of spring water
        and sprinkle it on a banana leaf;
the children think they hear rain
        starting to fall.

2.

The plums are so sour they make my teeth tingle.
Green banana leaves shade the gauze window.
A long day.... Mind empty of thoughts, I rise from my nap
and watch children chasing willow catkins.

UNTITLED

I watch a monkey climbing a tree.
The people below are afraid that he'll fall.
But the monkey swings smoothly from branch to branch,
and I feel like saying:
        "Don't worry about him!"

Watching a Village Festival

The village festival is really worth seeing—
mountain farmers praying for a good harvest.

Flute players, drummers burst forth from nowhere;
laughing children race after them.
Tiger masks, leopard heads swing from side to side.
Country singers, village dancers perform for the crowd.

I'd rather have one minute of this wild show
than all the nobility of kings and generals.

Feeling Lazy

My sleepy eyes fog over…long lazy day.
I put down my book of poetry
and take a walk around the house.
The cats are playing happily in the courtyard;
when they see me coming they scatter
        like frightened deer.

Drying Clothes

At noon I leave my clothes out to dry;
        at sunset I fold them up
and carry them home in a willow-wood box.
The women laugh and ask each other:
"Who's that old servant with bare feet?"

First Day of the Second Month: Rain and Cold

1.

I've patched all the windows and closed the doors;
the tea kettle and wine pot fill the room
        with a warm fragrance.
I tell my servant: "Don't sweep away
        the puddles in the courtyard:
I want to watch the raindrops making patterns."

2.

I comb my hair and sleep overcomes me:
I dream that all my white hairs are being cut.
I wake up: the wind is leaking through a crack in the window,
swinging a spider's web back and forth.

Night Rain at Kuang-k'ou

The river is clear and calm;
     a fast rain falls in the gorge.
At midnight the cold, splashing sound begins,
like thousands of pearls spilling onto a glass plate,
each drop penetrating the bone.

In my dream I scratch my head and get up to listen.
I listen and listen, until the dawn.
All my life I have heard rain,
     and I am an old man;
but now for the first time I understand
     the sound of spring rain
         on the river at night.

THE ILLUSTRATIONS

All the illustrations ae from the Chinese art collection of the late John M. Crawford, Jr.

Page 51: Ch'iu Ying (c. 1510–51), "Fisherman's Flute Heard Over the Lake," detail of hanging scroll; ink and faint colors on paper.

Page 52: T'ang Yin (1470–1523), "Drunken Fisherman by a Reed Bank," detail of hanging scroll; ink on paper.

Page 71: Chu Ta (c. 1625 to c. 1705), "Fish and Rocks," detail of hanging scroll; ink on paper.

Page 72: Wu Chen (1280–1354), "Fisherman," detail of hand scroll; ink on paper.

Page 91: Ma Yüan (late 12th to early 13th century), "Plum Blossoms by Moonight," album leaf; ink and color on silk.

Page 92: Unknown 12th-century artist, "River Hamlet," album leaf; ink and faint colors on silk.

Page 110: Wu-chun (c. 1175–1249), "Monk Riding a Mule," cropped top and bottom, hanging scroll; ink on paper.

Page 111: Liang K'ai (early 13th century), "Strolling on a Marshy Bank," album leaf; ink on silk.

JONATHAN CHAVES was born in New York in 1943. He received his Ph.D. in Chinese literature from Columbia University and is now professor of Chinese at the George Washington University in Washington, D.C. His translations of Chinese poetry have appeared in *The Hudson Review, Mademoiselle, New Letters, Transpacific, Granite,* and other literary magazines. He was guest curator of an exhibition of the relationship between poetry and painting in China, *The Chinese Painter as Poet,* at the China Institute in New York City in 2000.

Companions for the Journey Series

This series presents inspirational work by well-known writers
in a small-book format designed to be carried along
on your journey through life.

Volume 6
A Zen Forest: Zen Sayings
Translated by Soioku Shigematsu
Preface by Gary Snyder
1-893996-30-1   5 x 7   140 pages $14.00

Volume 5
Back Roads to Far Towns
Basho's Travel Journal
Translated by Cid Corman
1-893996-31-X   5 x 7   128 pages $13.00

Volume 4
Heaven My Blanket, Earth My Pillow
Poems from Sung Dynasty China by Yang Wan-Li
Translated by Jonathan Chaves
1-893996-29-8   5 x 7   120 pages $14.00

Volume 3
10,000 Dawns
The Love Poems of Claire and Yvan Goll
Translated by Thomas Rain Crowe and Nan Watkins
1-893996-27-1   5 x 7   96 pages $13.00

Volume 2

There Is No Road

Proverbs by Antonio Machado

Translated by Mary G. berg & Dennis Maloney

1-893996-66-2   5 x 7   120 *pages* $14.00

Volume 1

Wild Ways: Zen Poems of Ikkyu

Translated by John Stevens

1-893996-65-4   5 x 7   128 *pages* $14.00